Retirement-Age Policy

Pergamon Titles of Related Interest

Checkoway Citizens and Health Care: Participation and Planning for Social Change

Clark Effective Pension Planning: A Work in America Institute Study in Productivity

Rosow/Zager The Future of Older Workers in America: New Options for an Extended Working Life

Tamir Communication and the Aging Process: Interaction Throughout the Life Cycle

Tropman New Strategic Perspectives on Social Policy

Related Journals*

BULLETIN OF SCIENCE, TECHNOLOGY & SOCIETY
EVALUATION & PROGRAM PLANNING
SOCIAL SCIENCE AND MEDICINE
SOCIO-ECONOMY PLANNING SCIENCES
TECHNOLOGY IN SOCIETY

*Free specimen copies available upon request.

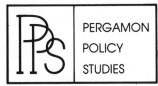

PERGAMON
POLICY
STUDIES

ON SOCIAL POLICY

Retirement-Age Policy
An International Perspective

Sara E. Rix
Paul Fisher

Pergamon Press

NEW YORK • OXFORD • TORONTO • SYDNEY • PARIS • FRANKFURT

Pergamon Press Offices:

U.S.A.	Pergamon Press Inc., Maxwell House, Fairview Park, Elmsford, New York 10523, U.S.A.
U.K.	Pergamon Press Ltd., Headington Hill Hall, Oxford OX3 0BW, England
CANADA	Pergamon Press Canada Ltd., Suite 104, 150 Consumers Road, Willowdale, Ontario M2J 1P9, Canada
AUSTRALIA	Pergamon Press (Aust.) Pty. Ltd., P.O. Box 544, Potts Point, NSW 2011, Australia
FRANCE	Pergamon Press SARL, 24 rue des Ecoles, 75240 Paris, Cedex 05, France
FEDERAL REPUBLIC OF GERMANY	Pergamon Press GmbH, Hammerweg 6 6242 Kronberg/Taunus, Federal Republic of Germany

Copyright © 1982 Pergamon Press Inc.

Library of Congress Cataloging in Publication Data
Rix, Sara E.
  Retirement-age policy.

  (Pergamon policy studies on social policy)
  Bibliography: p.
  1. Retirement age. I. Fisher, Paul, 1908-
II. Title. III. Series.
HD7105.R54   1982   306'.38   82-3730
ISBN 0-08-028840-5   AACR2

Printed in the United States of America

Contents

Foreword

Retirement-age policy was not a controversial issue in the United States in 1935 when age 65 was embodied in the Social Security Act. Today it is a highly controversial issue, and undoubtedly will continue to be one for a long time to come. Proposed changes in the retirement ages in social security are frequently discussed in some quarters in simplistic terms solely in relation to increased life expectancy. The subject, however, is more basically related to such other complex factors as employment, unemployment, economic growth, productivity, inflation, changing fertility rates, the overall dependency ratio (aged plus children), and all the allocation of changing resources in relation to changing priorities. There is a lot more we need to know before a precipitate policy decision is taken to raise or lower the retirement age for the United States. For instance, what should be the relationship between the retirement age policy in social security and private plans?

It is important to know what other advanced industrial countries have experienced, especially those with higher proportions of aged persons and long experience with social security and related programs under a variety of conditions. But national attitudes and institutions differ and should be given careful consideration in weighing policy and formulating program revisions in the United States.

The Rix-Fisher report is a provocative beginning in what should be a broad range of future studies needed to consider all the many facets of retirement-age policy. It should be carefully and critically studied by those who wish to play a participatory role in research and policy in the economic, political and social retirement-age issues during the coming decade.

Wilbur J. Cohen
Sid W. Richardson Professor of Public Affairs
L. B. J. School of Public Affairs
The University of Texas at Austin
Secretary of Health, Education, and Welfare, 1968

Acknowledgments

We wish to take this opportunity to thank the German Marshall Fund of the United States and the U.S. Administration on Aging for providing the funds to support this project on retirement-age policy. The assistance of Peter Weitz of the German Marshall Fund and Frances Jacobs of the Administration on Aging, which extended over many months, is particularly appreciated.

Many other people contributed in no small way to the completion of this manuscript. The idea for the study originated with Dr. Harold L. Sheppard, now with the National Council on the Aging, whose proposal secured funding for the study and who directed it in its earlier phases. He also must be thanked for his very thought-provoking introduction.

The project could not have been completed without the cooperation of experts in Europe who prepared working papers and conducted policy seminars on aging and retirement policy in their countries. These experts are Henning Friis and Per Vejrup Hansen of the Socialforskningsinstituttet in Denmark; Paul Paillat and Jean-Claude Chesnais of the Institut National d'Études Démographiques in France; Hans Berglind of the University of Stockholm and Alf Bergroth of the University of Östersund in Sweden; Harald Eichner and Klaus Grossjohann of the Gesellschaft für Sozialen Fortschritt in Germany; and Michael Fogarty of the Policy Studies Institute in the United Kingdom.

James Schulz of Brandeis University, George Rohrlich of Temple University, and Harold Sheppard reviewed an earlier draft of this book. Dorothy Edwards of the American Institutes for Research reviewed the final draft. Their reviews were sound, to the point, and often provided insights that we had overlooked. The expertise of these reviewers undoubtedly contributed to the final product. Any errors, of course, rest with the authors and not the reviewers.

As always, sincere thanks go to the project secretary, Doris Donohue, whose efforts on this cross-national study exceeded the call of duty. Brad Allen must be thanked for the long hours that he spent typing the final manuscript. Jeff Clair spent many productive hours as a research assistant on the project and as a coauthor of the U.S. working paper. The administrative assistance of John McDonald and Robert Archer is gratefully acknowledged.

Finally, it should be noted that both the German Marshall Fund and the Administration on Aging encourage grantees to express their judgment freely. This report does not necessarily reflect the opinion, or represent the policy, of either agency.

Introduction:
The Broad Context of
Retirement-Age Policy

Harold L. Sheppard

During the 1980s and certainly by the 1990s, the Western industrial societies will undoubtedly be confronting and debating (and to some extent, perhaps already "solving") their mutual problems associated with the growth of an "aging" population. Many of the sources of those problems are of a "short-term" nature—that is, primarily due to immediate, current surges in joblessness, inflation, and/or low or no productivity increases. Many other problem sources are of a much longer-term nature, although it could be argued that reality does not allow for a separation between short-term problem solutions and long-term problems. Short-term solutions have a way of creating longer-term problems and of affecting other preexisting long-term problems expected in the future.

This volume, authored by Sara Rix and Paul Fisher, concentrates on both the short- and long-term problems in five European countries (Denmark, France, West Germany, Sweden, and the United Kingdom) associated with the costs of supporting a rising population of retirees, particularly (but not exclusively) the costs of retirement income. The adjustments, the policy debates, and the policy responses among these five countries (and in the United States) have not been universal or similar. But neither are the conditions that characterize each of the countries—for example, mortality rates among adult and older persons, or attitudes about retirement itself.

In addition to variations in such matters, there remains the relatively unsettled issue as to whether we are undergoing a "biomedical revolution" that will lead to substantial strides in longevity. From my own point of view, in the United States, at least, we may be on the verge of such a radical change. This is evidenced by the frequent changes in official projections of the size of older age groups in our future population. These projections indicate a greater rate of increase in the numbers of Americans in their late seventies and older, than in other age groups, and greater than had been previously projected, which is the more vital point. This is brought about by sharp drops in the death rate in these and younger adult-age groups—drops that have been far greater than gerontologists and other experts had expected when writing in the 1960s and early 1970s about the future.

The main point here is that, contrary to the conventional wisdom of demography that fertility and migration were the key factors that varied enough to cause increases or decreases in a country's population size, we must now learn to cope with changes in adult mortality rates when trying to obtain a somewhat reasonable picture of what size our population 10, 15, or 20 years or more from now will be.

In any event, it is encouraging to see that some official demographers—after their estimates of future populations of older Americans repeatedly turned out to be *under*estimates when that future became reality—are now prepared to paint different population scenarios according to different mortality assumptions, and not just on the basis of different fertility and migration assumptions.

I have emphasized this point because, for one thing, we have tended to dismiss too cavalierly what appears on the surface as only slight increases in life expectancy for persons in their sixties or older. A "slight" increase in life expectancy for older persons, however, means an increase in *numbers* of older persons in the magnitude of hundreds of thousands, or millions, depending on the time span considered.

In 1971, the U.S. Census Bureau projected an elderly (65 and older) population for the year 2000 of 28.8 million. Six years later, their revisions, based on the then current mortality rates and life expectancies, cited not 28.8 million 65 and older, but 31.8 million. Three million more oldsters do not constitute a "slight increase."

Based on the unexpected but nevertheless real increase in life expectancies for older Americans from 1969 to 1979, more recent projections for the year 2000 now indicate that by that year we should expect to have more than 34 million. Within one decade, in other words, an additional 5 million or so older Americans in the future have been "found."

The implications of an older population of that size (34 million)—especially if thought of in the context of the size forecast in the early 1970s—are virtually without limits. By themselves, the numbers may mean little. But taken together with (a) continued early retirement trends, (b) high inflation, and (c) a low fertility rate, to cite only three factors, the question that arises and needs to be tackled, not evaded, is: Will the resulting costs involved become an intolerable burden on the economic institutions and the working population? What will be the reactions to that burden? Will they continue to be willing to endure the costs of that burden, especially if changes in their own incomes and standards of living are not commensurate with the changes in income and services received by a growing population of retirees?

In a very basic sense, Rix and Fisher are dealing in this book with an issue that is slowly coming to be conceptualized around the topic of the future of the Western European welfare state.

The progress toward a welfare state has, in large part, been possible, not simply as a result of an ideology, but as a result of a steadily improving economy capable of providing more and more in the way of retirement income and services for the elderly, as part of the general welfare state's largesse. Recent economic developments—stemming partly from the energy and resource crisis (which has become chronic)—have gone so far as to put a brake on any further progress (or to cast doubts on a continuation of that progress), even in that paragon of welfare states, Sweden (and its fellow Nordic Council nation, Denmark).

But in addition to, or apart from, these biomedical, demographic, and economic developments, there is also the fact that in such countries (including the United States), the *maturation* of retirement systems also has been a factor. By now, in most of the countries covered in the project, the bill has come due. As long as there are only a few workers retiring, with many other workers continuing to work and paying for the first group's retirement income, the challenge to the financing capacity of the system was nonexistent. But as the many workers "covered" by the system themselves begin to move into the ranks of the retired (and add their numbers to previous retirees who continue to live), and as the remaining working population—in proportion to the numbers now retired—diminishes in size, the strains on the system begin to show themselves. The demand for *adequate* pensions exerts further pressures.

Rix and Fisher deal primarily with five European countries' recent experiences with their own retirement systems' problems. But the one theme that might characterize what is happening in Denmark, France, West Germany, Sweden, and the United Kingdom, as well as the United States, is the *limits to the welfare state.*

At times, the much-touted "tax revolt" may be interpreted as a concrete sign that these countries are reaching such a limit. One does not have to be an arch-conservative to express this viewpoint. Gunnar Myrdal, the eminent Swedish social economist, is also concerned that in contemporary Western Europe (and by the same token, the United States), such "mature" industrial societies are experiencing a dilemma involving (1) persistent inflation, (2) high expectations of workers, consumers, and retirees, and (3) demographic changes that place heavy strains on their economies' capacities to meet all those expectations.

This new scenario is in marked contrast to the one that marked the three decades or so after World War II, especially since the 1950s. That period was generally marked by steadily rising personal consumption—including improvements in public welfare benefits—a rate and level of progress based on generally dynamic, growing economies.

What is at issue here is whether the economies during the rest of this century will be capable of providing *current*, let alone increased, levels of general welfare support (due partly to changing demographics but unchanging employment/retirement patterns), or will have to make major adjustments of one sort or another in their support systems.

By and large, the emergence of this type of challenge is not going to be affected significantly by the political makeup of a nation's leadership, although the responses to that challenge may be partly determined by political differences in that leadership. If, as in the United States today, the highest priority is placed on increasing drastically our defense budget "at all costs," and within a constrained total federal budget, budgets for social programs may undergo draconian reductions, and it appears that programs for an increasing aged retired population—even the previously sacrosanct social security program—may not escape such reductions.

The challenges of a growing older population, within a context of economic conditions (such as inflation, level of unemployment, economic growth) and biomedical developments, will be approached through a range of trade-off choices, but all of these—the economic conditions and biomedical developments, along with the range of choices—will, in all likelihood, be within a system or framework of constraints to any expansion of a "welfare state."

In general, economic growth makes it possible to finance increased social benefits and to set generous eligibility criteria. But this observation needs to be qualified: an early retirement policy can be either a partial result of society's economic well-being or a policy response to persistent high unemployment, as a way, it is believed, to reduce the unemployment rate and "make room" for younger workers. But early retirement is not cost-free, especially when greater longevity on the part of such retirees may be increasing.

The industrialized Western economies are all, to one extent or another, experiencing new limits to the growth of taxes, which is one part of the emergence of the "limits to the welfare state." To be sure, widespread complaints against taxes are especially rampant in a time of persistent, high inflation. Whether these complaints (or "tax revolts") are leveled on an across-the-board basis, or aimed at certain types of taxes more than others, is not always made clear in the media-based complaints. Our own U.S. information suggests that, contrary to popular media messages, some forms of taxes are less unpopular than others. Amazingly, when one considers the news and editorial contents of the media, in America at least, Americans complain *less* about paying social security taxes than other forms. This is not a prediction, however, that *decreases* or freezes in some or all social security program benefits will be resisted by sufficient numbers of Americans. Despite what they may respond in opinion surveys, many citizens may be happy that national leaders will make the decision for them, without feeling that they were responsible.

In all of the countries covered in our project, a backlash against social expenditures—a taxpayers' revolt—is developing in one form or another. A European Community survey in the early 1970s found, for example, that the

British had the toughest attitude about poverty among the several member countries of the European Community.

Furthermore, as Michael Fogarty tells us, the Conservative Party "has shown a particular interest in limiting direct taxation," and this includes social security, presumably to create a more favorable environment for investments by the private sector. But even the Labour government cut back public expenditures as a percent of gross domestic product, and the Conservative government has worked to reduce the percentage even more. Under the current Reagan regime, even the Democrats have become sensitive to welfare-cost issues.

But is there really a tax revolt? The answer is a cloudy one. Just as in the United States, where politicians and journalists talk and act as if there is one, in the face of public opinion polls suggesting the contrary, in the United Kingdom and elsewhere, it appears that a willingness to pay *more* taxes if necessary to extend health, education, and welfare might even be increasing. From 1979 to 1980, two Gallup polls found that the proportion of the British public approving of increases in taxes rose from 34 percent to 48 percent.

One of the ironies, or paradoxes, in the present situation of the welfare state in Western Europe is that while the recent poor economic performance has led to a greater focus on unemployment problems, as the need to solve this problem increased, the governments have become "increasingly reluctant to commit themselves to the provision of adequate resources." "The greater the need, the less the capacity" is the maxim cited by a London School of Economics observer (Taylor, 1980).

Even West Germany is now being forced to come to grips with challenges to its own welfare state. Its enviable economic growth rate of recent years is being thwarted, partly because of a worsening of its export position and greater demands for an increased defense budget, "narrowing the margin of the public household available for transfer payments" (Alber, 1980).

While the "pensioners peak" in Germany will ease during the present decade, there is a radically changing demographic trend which will keep the aged population at very high levels. It will assume serious dimensions when the small number of persons born in the 1970s enter the labor force. This will aggravate the real dependency ratio, since the retired population—given no change in current retirement age policy—will be even greater in the not so distant future. Germany's fertility record is well below "replacement rate."

In this respect, then, the future of the welfare state is more than a function of economic growth, unless the growth is of such a magnitude as to compensate for a growing dependency ratio. A wealthy, prosperous economy can afford high dependency ratios.

It is easier to talk in the abstract about the limits of tax burdens, or of the welfare state, than to specify exactly where or when the limits are reached in actual fact.

Jens Alber reminds us that the history of this type of debate suggests that we have had, many times in the past, flat declarations that the limits had already been reached, or were about to be reached. "Time and again, the development of the welfare state has surpassed previously maintained limits to growth or allegedly unbearable thresholds of the burden of costs." This reminds us of the 150 years of endless predictions of the end of capitalism itself among orthodox, classical Marxists, predictions which live to be contradicted by reforms and adaptations of and by capitalist economies and governments. This should not, however, become a source of overcomplacency as far as retirement-age trends and pension levels are concerned.

According to Alber, "where the actual limits lie is probably more a question of the governments' capacity to mobilize political support for their social policies than of 'objective' economic conditions." But even the public is capable of adapting to difficult "objective" economic conditions. In 1978, Alber reports, 71 percent of the general public in Germany (and even 56 percent of retirees) accepted the possibility of reduced growth rates in pensions in future years.

When it comes to justifying such a policy, it may prove more practical to explain to the public the relationship between rising costs and decreasing resources than to couch the justification in ideological rhetoric about the evils of a growing state or government and the virtues of self-reliance and "individual freedom."

In the United States, broad-gauged economists—those concerned about general economic conditions and problems, such as Lester Thurow (who is no conservative)—are now arguing that the time may have come to slow down the growth of social security benefits. Thurow (1981) says it is not good economics and not good politics to add to the income of the elderly (or keep its purchasing power intact), while the average worker's real income is declining. At the very least, pleads Thurow, benefits should grow only at the same pace as the wages of the population that pays the taxes to provide those benefits: "We all live in the same economy, and we should all prosper or suffer depending on its performance."

There is some evidence that senior citizens would accept this philosophy. Surveys sponsored by the American Association of Retired Persons show that most of them would prefer to see a slowdown in inflation—despite their own relative immunity from its effects.

Sooner or later, the United States will adopt a more flexible approach, as some of the European countries have done, to the issue of protecting social security benefits against inflation, and probably along the lines of Thurow's position. Every democratic government reaches a point in its policy and budget decisions at which it must act as a representative of the working population, as well as of the nonworking retired population.

In May 1981, the United States Senate voted to change the reference base for adjusting retirees' benefits (including those of federal government retirees) from the exclusive reliance on the Consumer Price Index (CPI) to a base on either that index or on the national average rate of change in *wages*, whichever is lower. The vote on this controversial issue (which, like the retirement-age issue, is fraught with emotions among organized senior citizen groups) was along almost strictly political party lines. Only 14 percent of the Senate Democrats, contrasted to 90 percent of the Republicans, voted to shift to the new method.

Whether the proposal is enacted into law is not the point here. The point is that the issue is emerging on the formal, legislative stage sooner than anyone would have predicted, say, in late 1980, when both political parties and their presidential candidates pledged to keep sacrosanct the CPI-based inflation-protection ingredient of pensioners' benefits. When budget directors and legislators put on their green eyeshades of pristine economic rationality, nothing, it appears, remains sacred. This is a statement that needs some qualification or correction, however.

1. Such a sharp policy turnaround is also based on political perceptions. To repeat what I said earlier, governments—elected officials especially—represent the larger electorate of contributors to, and not merely the recipients of, retirement income benefits.

2. In this respect, the case for such a turnabout can be based on the equity argument—that is, fairness. If the contributions are based on earnings, benefits based on prices, in extended periods in which earnings lag seriously behind prices, the conditions for "ressentiment" can accumulate toward a breaking point.

We are thereby faced with a clear-cut example of value conflicts. This argument about equity can be countered by advocates for the aged; for example, by the defensible claim that retired workers contributed, when they were employed for 35 or more years, to the economic well-being of today's workers, who should therefore be willing to make some temporary sacrifices until the inflation crisis recedes.

There is obviously an urgent need for policies enhancing employment growth, and for general economic well-being. But Fogarty (1980b) feels that, for Great Britain in the early 1980s, "the climate for the elderly is clearly cold. Two successive governments of different parties have severely squeezed public expenditure [which] has created a very cold climate indeed for claims for further improvements in social security pensioners' rights. . . . In local authorities' housing and personal social services and in the National Health Service the squeeze has raised a serious question whether existing standards of service can be maintained as the numbers of the very elderly rise." These remarks may be applied to other societies, too.

As for the mid-1980s, Fogarty becomes a little more optimistic, and he discusses three propositions and assumptions about conditions between now and the end of the century which are clearly on the optimistic side of the scales: (1) the British economy will again be under control; (2) job opportunities will be open to all who want them; and (3) moderate growth in real income will be possible (Fogarty, 1980b).

Fogarty's viewpoint is tempered, of course, by his expectation that there will be greater competition for funds for the benefit of other groups, not just the elderly, at a time when the "very old" (75 and older) will be a growing proportion of the general older population, thus increasing the need for services support of a more costly nature. Fogarty himself warns that there will probably have to be greater variety or diversification in the *sources* of retirement income, although there is no certainty that private pensions can sufficiently solve the problem. Even though the government will always be the main source, "the more that can be found through other channels the better will be the prospects not only for pensioners but also for other groups against which pensioners (however distasteful they and their interest groups may find it) have inevitably to compete for public funds" (Fogarty, 1980b).

Such a statement is again another way of talking about the limits of the Western welfare state during the rest of this century and possibly into the next.

France, too, may be moving into a "cold climate." Before the Second World War, France had a system based largely on funded pensions; but because that country's inflation problems became so serious, the government then moved to a system of *repartition*—essentially a pay-as-you-go method for meeting pension obligations. Paillat and Chesnais (1980) report that this new method "made it possible to pay pensions to retired workers who had not previously contributed to the fund." But as the program reached its mature level, the ratio of contributors to pensioners began to exert a negative effect. The deterioration of that ratio, Paillat and Chesnais claim, was obscured by a relatively long period of prosperous economic growth. With the poor economic conditions of today, however, coupled with a sharp drop in the fertility rate in France, the effects of the change in the ratio can no longer be ignored as it was during the good years of economic growth.

As in other countries, the chronic recessions can bring about an increased rate of retirement. They raise the question: In the long run, is such a trend bearable without impairing too much economic dynamism, for instance, by an excessive load on productive capital?

Despite the spotlight thrown by the media on the issue and the predictions by experts of a fast-growing intergenerational conflict, it remains a fact, as suggested earlier, that the role of government in assuring economic security in old age, even if it means higher costs, still ranks high in our own public opinion polls here in the United States.

None of this, however, should detract from the expectation that by the end of this century, and *despite* the scheduled 1985 and 1990 social security payroll tax increases, estimated revenues for that system will be inadequate to meet the needs for expenditures by the old age and survivors trust fund in the early years of the twenty-first century—less than two decades away.

Even these estimates may be on the conservative side if, as discussed in Rix and Fisher's second chapter, the social security population projections are on the low side due to a reluctance to accept the possibility of even lower mortality rates among older adult groups. This obviously would produce far greater numbers of elderly Americans, most of them on the nonworking side of the dependency ledger.

Returning to the optimistic scenario, such as that portrayed by Fogarty, other qualifications or reservations include the issue of encouraging retirement on a pension—versus work continuity—by the "young old." This is an issue that I have discussed in the context of a value system that emphasizes the priority of assuring a decent standard of retirement living for the very old—the fastest growing aged segment for most, if not all, of the six countries in this project. Given that value position, it may be even more incumbent upon the *young old* to continue to work, alongside members of the younger working population, to share with them the costs of providing that decent standard of retirement life for their older peers—and in order to assure the same status when they themselves become members of the very-old generation. Given the rising life expectation among the young old, they have an even greater stake in such a policy than do the current cohort of the very old.

Early retirement, which includes "retirement" below pensionable age, can and does result not merely from the "supply side" (availability of pensions below "normal" retirement age), but also from a drop in demand for workers, namely, unemployment. But the step toward early (and earlier) retirement—regardless of reason, regardless of who initiates it (government, employee, or employer)—can set new patterns that would prove difficult to reverse. "It would be risky to assume that, if employment recovered, activity rates among older men would simply return to the trend which prevailed till the middle of the 1970s" (Fogarty, 1980b).

This underscores the proposition that short-term solutions cannot be presumed not to have long-term carry-overs and implications. Early retirement policies are not like a water faucet that can be turned on and off in immediate response to changing conditions and needs.

The special early retirement scheme in the United Kingdom—the Job Release Scheme, introduced in early 1977 as a response to high unemployment—accounts for no more than one-fifth of retirements among persons 60–64. Nevertheless, the United Kingdom analysts believe that early retirement will continue, and continue at an increasing pace—at least among men—largely because of the growing attractiveness of the occupational (private) pension benefit levels.

This type of information and forecast is the basis for Fogarty's critique of the conventional dependency-ratio measure, which, if accepted uncritically, provides a "favorable picture of the prospective balance in Britain between the active and the inactive population."

While much of the focus of our earlier work on the United States (Sheppard and Rix, 1977) was on early retirement age as an issue, and on prolonging working life as one of the major solutions to the pension-cost problem, Rix and Fisher point out that suggestions for raising retirement age in the five European countries were not proposed as frequently as in America. To be sure, the issue of the future costs of their respective pension and service program for the elderly is preoccupying European public policymaking activities as much as they are in the United States.

One reason, perhaps, for the relative lack of emphasis on raising retirement age is that for some countries, there is no apparent increase in the conventionally measured "dependency ratio" (even though *costs* are the more important measure). Another, more readily understood reason is the immediate, short-term issue of unemployment. This condition has led their governments—but especially the trade unions—to concentrate, not on the *long-run implications* of current retirement age trends and policies (in the context of expected demographic and economic trends), but on *solutions* to the immediate problems of joblessness. One of those proposed solutions has been to reduce even further the retirement age—ostensibly, in some cases, on only a temporary basis.

This explanation, however, does not help us understand why it is, during recent high-unemployment periods in the United States, serious proposals to lower the social security retirement age as a way of "solving" the problem of high joblessness never surfaced among United States labor unions.

In all of the contemporary discussions and literature dealing with changes in the retirement age, it is apparently assumed or taken for granted that the changes have always been downward, toward an earlier-pension-age policy. But the Danish record shows a different story. Friis and Hansen report, in the Danish document for this project, that in 1937 a coalition government of Social Democrats and Radicals reduced the age limit to 60, as a policy response to the depression conditions at that time. But immediately after the Second World War, a different government (under the Agricultural or Farmers Party) *raised* the age for men to 65; and by 1956 (under the trade-union-backed Social Democrats, no less) enacted a gradual increase for men to age 67 and for women from 60 to 62.

The further significance of this upward age policy shift lies in the fact that an argument that is being articulated in the United States today was expressed then, a quarter of a century ago: that the duration of life has been increasing; people do not get old as early as they did before. Again, this reasoning was put forward, not by a conservative spokesman for industry nor by an "expert," but by a leader of the Social Democrats.

The point of all this is that there are precedents for raising the age of retirement in Western Europe and that many of the European countries apparently are capable of considering new upward adjustments. Furthermore, as I have suggested throughout this introduction, the United States now stands on the threshold of the same type of decision. What was once a footnote in official and technical reports is now surfacing in the 1980s in leading national opinion-influencing publications through editorials and, more important, in serious congressional proposals: a change in retirement age, and upward.

The *Wall Street Journal*, on June 26, 1980, for example, highlighted the Presidential Commission on Pension Policy's recommendation to raise the age of eligibility for retirement under social security. For the *Journal*, "this move is the simplest way of easing the expected troubles of retirement programs." The editorial stated that "much as we might celebrate the opportunities our society offers for long and rewarding retirements, it is important to realize that retirement benefits impose high costs on the rest of the economy, and that unless our policies change, those costs will soon grow much more burdensome."

In the same month, a *New York Times* editorial ("The Toll of the Pension Clock") also pointed to the growing notion that "the social security burden could be reduced by raising the eligibility age to reflect increasing life expectancy." After the presidential election of 1980, a November editorial in the same influential paper stressed that the Pension Commission staff's recommendations to raise retirement age from 65 to 68 (instead of still higher payroll taxes or reduced benefits) "is hardly a radical idea." Average life expectancy has increased by much more than three years since social security began; thus a three-year extension in retirement age would not deprive future beneficiaries of leisure time available to their predecessors. Nor would anyone over the age of 45 be affected, since the change would not have to take effect until the turn of the century.

Among the several choices before us as ways to meet the longer-term financial problems of the social security system, there may not be one clearly and obviously easy solution. "What is clear," concludes the June 1980 *New York Times* editorial, "is that the country would be better off debating the issue now, while there is time to make gradual changes, rather than later when the crisis is upon us."

The August 25, 1980 issue of *Fortune* magazine published an article on "How to Save Social Security," by A.F. Ehrbar. For that writer, there would be no need for raising the social security payroll tax over the rate now scheduled by the end of this decade, if, in addition to a change in the benefit formula, the full benefit retirement age were raised from 65 to 68—again, starting in the year 2000.

The *Fortune* article cites a National Bureau of Economic Research study's calculation of the effect of raising the retirement age to 68: "a $200 billion surplus in the old-age portion of the system." If 68 were the "full-benefits" retirement age, it is estimated that nearly three-fourths of the fund's long-term deficit would be eliminated. Ehrbar, too, emphasizes that such a change does not mean any reduction in retirement years, compared to those for retirees of the past, because of the increased life expectancy of older Americans.

Saving the social security system itself and preserving it as a viable institution into the next century obviously means departures from what individuals may have planned or expected, although it is not clear whether any worker in his or her early forties today believes that an increase to age 68 for full-benefit eligibility is an abrogation of a commitment made to him or her. Advocates of an increase in retirement age point out that if the retirement age shift is rejected, then other, perhaps more objectionable alternatives, such as reduced benefits or increased taxes, must be confronted and considered.

Of course, a high employment and economic-growth rate leaves many options open. A society could then provide more money to the retirees, allow more people to retire, or develop job opportunities for more older workers.

A congressional Joint Economic Committee (JEC), in a November 1980 report, links economic growth and social security. Its chairman, Senator Lloyd Bentson, states what should be clear to all:

> Retirement benefits are being threatened by inflation, unemployment, and lagging productivity. If we revitalize our economy, we will have taken a long step toward restoring faith in our retirement programs. . . . Increasing employer-employee contributions will only make things worse by discouraging economic expansion.

The report presents the startling cost of unemployment to the social security system: for every one million unemployed workers each month in 1980, the system lost $100 million in contributions. The same JEC report stresses the viewpoint that the "future potential GNP may not be realized unless older Americans are encouraged to continue working."

In the same month that this JEC report was released, a key and influential advisor to President Reagan, Casper Weinberger, advocated in a nationwide television talk show that "working on" was justified because of the longer life span of Americans and because of a growing desire (need?) of individuals to work beyond age 65.

By the Spring of 1981, even a subcommittee on social security, with a Democratic majority, tentatively voted for a proposal to raise, on a gradual basis, the full-benefit social security retirement age to age 68 by the year 2000. This is a far cry from the earlier unwillingness of Congress to even whisper such an option as a major way of meeting the longer-term problem of keeping the social security system on a sound financial basis.

The typical demographic approach to the issues now being examined and debated tells us little about the costs associated with providing income and services for a population of retirees. It is the cost issue, not the body count, that underlies the debate. The body-count perspective is by itself insufficient, as long as it ignores such factors as the following:

1. Actual retirement age
2. Pension benefit levels
3. The level of inflation growth and whether, and to what degree, benefits are adjusted in accordance with that growth
4. Life expectancy after actual retirement age
5. The age composition of the "elderly" population, which affects the costs of services

On this last point, the American Office of Management and Budget (OMB), under the Carter Administration, had been taking a long and in-depth look at the implications of the "aging of the aged," particularly the cost impact of a disproportionate growth in the numbers of Americans roughly 80 and older. This is the population that, for example, requires, more than other age groups, an inordinate degree of costly long-term care. While the 85-plus population grew by 133 percent from 1950 to 1970, those of the same age group in institutions increased by more than 400 percent. The same pattern persists now, and may in the future. Among the noninstitutionalized oldest population, disability rates are more than twice those for persons 75–84 and four times as great as among those only 65–74. Even if we focus narrowly on only the medical needs involved, according to OMB sources, the $8 billion spent in 1980 could mount to as much as $25 billion by 1990. Other types of needed services associated with long-term care are much higher in costs.

All of this brings us back to the need to develop employment, economic growth, and retirement-age policies that can provide the wherewithal to meet such cost challenges. In this instance, as in so many other dimensions of the issues associated with aging, the decisions arrived at affect all of us. We are talking about our "future selves." Part of that wherewithal may require the retention of the "young old"—those around 60–69 years old—in the labor force, to enhance the labor base on the contributing side, rather than the recipient side, of the ledger.

The British trade union push for retirement for everyone at age 60 (already the age for women) includes the insistence that there would be no actuarial reduction. In other words, the pension at 60 would be the same as it is now for workers retiring at age 65. Estimates by the government indicate a cost of £3.6 billion a year for the state-run scheme, not counting costs to the private (occupational) plans—which tend to change their pension ages in accordance with social security.

Other proposals in the United Kingdom concerning changes in the retirement age call for an age halfway between the 60 for women and the 65 for men, although the Trades Union Congress (TUC) opposes raising the age for women. Estimates of the costs point to a slight increase, depending on the precise age settled upon, but the National Association of Pension Funds believes that by the end of this century, a common retirement age of 63 could be possible at no cost. (For explanation and details of this cost, see Fogarty, 1980b.)

Fogarty's report on the United Kingdom presents the quantitative/demographic shift toward the very old (75 and older) in the British population projections. He points to forecasts by Benjamin/Overton (1980) of a very large, disproportionate increase in the 75-plus population on the basis of substantially augmented service costs if geriatric standards are accepted and implemented.

The age at which a government permits workers to retire with a pension is not completely a result of caprice or social convention—at least not at the time the pension system itself is created. Certainly, life expectancy needs to be taken into consideration, particularly the life expectancy of a worker at the age of his or her retirement. Germany provides an interesting example: its Old Age Security Act of nearly a century ago set the pension age at 70. But so few workers lived to be that age, and if they did, had very few retirement years to look forward to. Nearly 30 years after the original act, the pensionable age was reduced to 65.

It is by now an old wives' tale that our own age for full pension eligibility under social security was selected at 65 partly because of Germany's selection of that age in 1916. But life expectancy for older workers has increased dramatically since 1916—and since 1935, the year in which our own social security system was enacted.

Suppose we accept the less-than-optimistic position that by the next 20 years or so, we will be forced to come to grips with the retirement-age policy issue—because of the unacceptable costs involved. What are the options that should be talked and thought about now if we do *not* take seriously the current proposals to raise the retirement age? The chapters in this book devoted to the range of "remedies" for the solvency problem of social security and the extension of working life may be the authors' most important contributions.

The first thing that needs saying is that the widely accepted position that it is not worthwhile to discuss options now (since economic, biomedical, and demographic projections about the future are too "iffy") may be used too often—and against our own good—as an excuse or rationale for not looking into the future in order to lay out, now, what the options could be in the event of, say, the most "pessimistic" scenario actually coming to be the case 10, 15, 20 or more years from now.

As Rix and Fisher state it, if we keep putting off any serious discussions for this reason, "social security pension planning, which must take into account the long-run development of earnings, employment, demographic changes, and so forth, is badly served." This observation applies to all the six countries in which we have been interested, though Rix and Fisher assert that the European societies have an extra problem of being more heavily dependent on exports than is the United States.

What are those options that I have culled from discussions and the literature? Without attempting to be encyclopedic, let me list the options, keeping in mind that no one of them can singly meet the challenge.

1. We could save a great deal of public expenditures for retirement income if we restricted payment of taxpayer (or worker) contributions to only those elderly who can truly prove that without such retirement income payments, they could not survive or provide themselves an "adequate" standard of living.

2. We could simply impose, on top of those payroll taxes (increases already scheduled between now and after the turn of the century), *additional* payroll taxes (and/or increases in the maximum ceiling of earnings that are taxed).

3. Instead of raising such taxes or contributions, we could reduce the benefits, or at least lower the rate of increase in those benefits.

4. Policies leading to the greater labor force participation—on more of a full-time basis—of women could be put into effect. This would add to the "support base" needed to provide the necessary expenditures for rising retirement income and elderly services costs.

5. Along the same lines, for the same purpose of adding to the support base, we could add other groups of workers not currently contributing to the basic retirement-income source (for example, federal government employees in the United States or in Germany and France).

6. The general income-tax system could be used to supplement the earmarked retirement-income system.

7. The formula for pension cost-of-living benefit adjustments (especially those automatically provided) could be adjusted *downward*.

8. More of the funding could be shifted away from a pay-as-you-go (transfer payment) system to a "capital" and/or advance funding system.

These options, to repeat, are alternatives to the change in retirement age that are emerging—at least in the United States. Some of these alternatives warrent comments, and I would argue that the most objectionable policy is the first one, namely, providing retirement income for only the "truly needy." Despite the growing theme of the Reagan administration's welfare philosophy that stresses the notion that too many Americans are living off of hard-working American taxpayers, and *unnecessarily*, it is not certain that when push comes to shove, such an approach would be easily salable when it comes to abandoning the philosophy of the nearly half-century-old social security system. It might be far more preferable to tax half the social security benefits of retirees (derived from the employer contribution). At least this could result in the lowest-income elderly not having to pay any taxes at all, in keeping with the progressive nature of income tax schedules. Many European countries have long followed this practice.

As for raising the payroll tax, it could be argued that both here and in Europe, the public—as suggested in polls—would accept having to pay more taxes (or accept smaller wage increases) in order to assure an adequate retirement standard of living for the elderly. But as in all phenomena, there looms the principle of limits. How *much* would they actually be willing to pay? If, as appears likely, workers' real incomes lag behind, or remain only even with, a continuing high inflation rate while the purchasing power of retirees' state-derived incomes is assured through cost-of-living adjustments (paid for through taxes on workers), how long might those opinion polls continue to show a strong intergenerational "social contract"?

And, as I have suggested above, would the public really accept new and large increases in such taxes? Governments, after all, represent the working population as well as those not working. And despite the touted influence of the "gray lobby," this does not mean that politicians, employers, and trade union officials can ignore, at all costs, the views of the working population.

I have not listed here, as an option, the argument that we might rely on the lower fertility rate to lighten the overall support load—that the increased size of the retired aged population will be compensated by a decreased child population. Fertility, family planning, or birth control (or their opposites) are not exactly susceptible to direct governmental policy decisions. Family size is a function of many social, psychological, and personal economic variables not so easily influenced by legislation or fiat.

In any event, a decrease in the number of children roughly equal to an increase in the number of nonworking elderly does not mean an equal trade-off as far as costs are concerned. And in just less than two decades or so, what was once the smaller child population becomes a smaller labor-force-entry population at the very time that the size of the nonworking elderly population continues to swell. West Germany provides one of the most extreme examples of this phenomenon; it could be said that in that country, the gastarbeiter population—if their own native lands continue to have relatively high birthrates—will assume an increasingly indispensable role as a complement to the extremely small work-force-entry population of young Germans within the next 20 years.

While there is a growing trend toward greater paid employment (higher labor-force participation) among women in most countries, we have to keep in mind at least three points:

1. For a long time to come, the proportion of full-time, year-round employed women will not suffice to be a one-to-one offset to the declining participation rate among men.

2. So far, even among full-time, year-round women workers, their earnings are *below* those of men also employed on a year-round, full-time basis; again, this means no one-to-one replacement as a base for payroll contributions into a fund used to pay for the pensions of the retired—mostly men.

3. There is the "maturity" principle: eventually these supporters become dependents, swelling the rolls of the already retired.

The use of general revenues has the attraction attributed to it by such analysts as Harold Wilensky, namely, their "invisibility"—as contrasted, say, to a payroll tax explicitly earmarked for paying pensions to the already retired. Its use, of course, would result in a redistribution of the sources (such as unearned income) to pay for part of the general pension. But it does not change the aggregate cost.

The option dealing with proposals for changing the base or formula for "inflation indexing" (to reduce costs) is considered elsewhere in this introduction. Suffice it to say at this point that the option is no longer an "academic" one.

Retirement-Age Policy

1

The Future of
Retirement-Age Policy

Suppose, for a moment, that the news media reported the development of a cure for cardiovascular disease. The discovery would be hailed by all, and especially by those over 60, whose leading cause of death would thereby be eliminated. Millions more could look forward to a long retirement life, until struck down by cancer, accident, or failure of some vital organ.

But how would the country support those millions, when in 1980 it took the social security taxes of nearly three workers to pay the benefits of just one retiree?

Nothing so dramatic as this medical breakthrough is likely to happen in the foreseeable future, but we should not ignore the hard fact that less striking medical breakthroughs have led to declining mortality rates at older ages. The development of effective birth-control measures, coupled with economic pressures and fear of overpopulation, has led to a declining birthrate. The joint result: a growing proportion of the population is in the 65-or-older age group, many of whom are living to very old age. Financial support of this older age group comes primarily from public and private retirement funds, and earlier retirement age and/or longer life span increases the number of years an individual must be supported by such funds. At the very upper ages, support costs—because of the high cost of health care—may be especially pronounced. This epitomizes the moral of our story.

Concern exists, in the United States at least, that a rapidly expanding aged and retired population will place such severe financial strains on workers and retirement funds that without drastic tax increases, the latter will be unable or no longer willing to ensure an adequate level of retirement support for elders. These concerns were the subject of *The Graying of Working America: The Coming Crisis in Retirement Age Policy*. Published in 1977 (Sheppard and Rix), this book deals with the cost implications of current trends in U.S. retirement-age policy at a time when the economic and demographic structure of the country was (and still is) undergoing significant changes. Similar changes characterize many other industrialized nations.

1

AN AGING POPULATION

One of the more identifiable trends in Western Europe, as in the United States, is the increase in the aged component of the population. The consequences of this development have been widely discussed and debated. One effect that is fairly well documented involves the growth of transfer payments—social security in particular—to an increasing number of retired workers.

The number of benefit payments has been affected, not only by an absolute increase in the number of persons above "normal" pensionable age, but also by a growing trend toward early retirement. Extension of pension protection to more segments of the population has further increased the number of pension benefits, while mortality improvements among men and women have extended the period of time over which benefits must be paid. Moreover, the pension benefit amount (in real terms) has grown substantially, due to the maturation of pension systems, the liberalization of benefit formulae, and indexing (inflation-proofing). The growth of the very old (75-plus) as a percentage of the total older population has, in addition, increased expenditures for the health care and social services required by this age group.

In the near future, and even more so after the turn of the century, the shift in the age structure of the population is likely to lead to a labor force with a greater percentage of middle-aged and older workers. If this is not offset by other developments, an aging labor force, it is often speculated, will lead to reduced productivity, reduced innovation, and, in some countries, ultimately to a small labor force. The changes in the age distribution of the population and the labor force would affect not only the manpower supply, but also the composition and magnitude of domestic demand for goods and services.[1]

All of this begs the question as to whether the economies of industrialized nations have—or will have in coming decades—the capacity to meet additional pressures such as the projected continuing aging of the population, an increase in the number and proportion of workers opting for early retirement, or demands for higher benefits and more extensive social services programs, *without* a corresponding decline in personal consumption. Some Swedish economists, for example, express the view that, assuming current demographic trends and no change in current labor force, personal consumption will indeed have to decline to ensure adequate support for the retired population (Sheppard, 1978).

Like the United States, the industrialized nations of Western Europe are undergoing socioeconomic, demographic, and biomedical developments that *may* threaten public support for a variety of welfare and income-transfer programs, including those for the aged and retired.

The ability to provide a vast array of medical and social services, as well as financial support, was made possible, at least in part, by the unprecedented post–World War II economic development that guaranteed an increase in personal consumption. As long as wages rise faster than prices or taxes, or as long as tax brackets are adjusted for inflation, support for expanding welfare programs *may* be assured. But whether such auspicious circumstances will characterize the future is debatable.

Slower growth, high inflation, and rising unemployment are problems facing many Western European nations at present. At the same time, recent trends in fertility, mortality, and early retirement have generated concern in some Western European circles that the population of working age will be forced to shoulder an unreasonably large tax burden to provide for aged and retired citizens.

Such an outcome is by no means inevitable. Productivity increases could, for example, foster a continued rise in the standard of living. Inflation rates might be moderated. A significant increase in fertility, stepped-up immigration, and/or a sharp increase in the number of working women could serve as an offset to any burden resulting from recent demographic trends. Projected aged support burdens might be relieved by restraining the rate of growth of services to, and programs for, dependent groups, or by actually cutting back services and benefit levels.

Taxpayers, too, might willingly accept a substantially higher tax load, especially if this guarantees—or appears to guarantee—that programs in which they have a vested interest will be available when they need them. Attitudes about the government's role in promoting public welfare undeniably differ among nations. Hence, the public's response to any economic burden associated with an aging population should be examined within the relevant cultural context. Welfare states, such as Denmark and Sweden, may be much more receptive than other countries to increased taxes for social and public-assistance programs.

Even in the United States, which can hardly be classified as a welfare state, one finds fairly widespread agreement that certain favored groups, of which the elderly are one, must be adequately protected against income inadequacy. Some public-opinion polls have revealed a clear preference for higher social security taxes over the alternative consisting of lower benefits to current and future retirees. Nonetheless, in the United States and perhaps even in the so-called welfare states, there may be a point beyond which support costs become so pronounced that even the most acceptable dependent groups fall out of favor.

The inquiry in this book focuses on the magnitude of the aged dependency burden, and on perceptions of that burden, in five European countries—Denmark, France, Sweden, West Germany, and the United Kingdom. Each of these countries is, to one degree or another, confronted with demographic and economic developments and problems comparable to those in the United States.

Each of them is experiencing growing demands on retirement income systems, due in part to past commitments, more recent liberalization of early retirement eligibility criteria, and/or the provision of pensions to a greater

number of people (for instance, France recently extended compulsory coverage through the "general system" to all self-employed workers.)

Simultaneously, a growing ratio of pension beneficiaries to contributors
has been observed in some pension systems, a trend that is likely to continue
with slight fluctuations up to and beyond the year 2000.[2] In Germany, for
example, the ratio of beneficiaries to contributors in its blue-collar pension
system increased by almost one-third (from 0.535:1 to 0.704:1) between 1970
and 1975 alone. By the turn of the century, it will take the contributions of
nearly two active workers to finance the needs of one retired person. During
the same period (1970–1975) in Sweden, the number of old-age pensioners
increased by 12 percent and the number of disability pensioners by over 50
percent.

According to the director of the Caisse Nationale Vieillesse de la Sécurité
Sociale in France, the ratio of workers to retirees dropped from 4:1 to 3:1
between 1969 and 1978. In the French railroad industry (SNCF)—where
workers can retire as early as 50 and others at 55—the burden of pension
costs is clear: pension payments consume the equivalent of more than 50
percent of the wages of workers employed in that industry (Sheppard, 1978).
Income-maintenance, health, and social-service programs and the like constitute a substantial share of social expenditures in these countries. In Sweden, for example, one-third of all social expenditures go to pensioners, including those on disability (Berglind and Bergroth, 1980). About half of all
public expenditures in France involved social expenditures in 1978; the elderly ranked first with 40 percent of the total (Paillat and Chesnais, 1980). Of
the £15.4 billion social security budget in the United Kingdom, 54 percent
was spent on the aged. (Other social security expenditures were for sickness,
unemployment, and family allowances.) Although the United Kingdom's
65-and-older population comprised 14 percent of the total population in
1977, 38 percent of all health and social-service expenditures went to them
(Fogarty, 1980a).

The potential consequences of projected further demands on pension systems and other programs and services benefiting the elderly are not lost to
policymakers in these European countries. In several (France, Sweden, and
West Germany), high-level commissions have been appointed to examine
these developments.[3] Our interest, as developed in this book, centered specifically around the extent to which recent and projected economic, demographic, and biomedical developments have resulted in a reevaluation of programs
and policies for the aged, particularly with respect to a sharp increase in
contributions and/or a reduction in benefits, the latter possibly achieved by
a higher retirement age. Quite simply, is a higher retirement age being considered as one, even partial, mechanism to alleviate the growing aged support
burden in these five European countries?

Subsequent chapters deal primarily with the findings of a study of the
future of retirement-age policy in five European countries confronted with

the problems of aging populations and, wherever indicated, with reference to similar problems in the United States.[4]

These chapters highlight both the extent to which the five countries are aging and th: problems created by this development, coupled with others such as little or no productivity progress, above-average unemployment and inflation rates, declining fertility, and early retirement trends. The short- and long-term consequences of these developments are discussed in some detail.

The data in the following chapters point to one thing: each of the countries has experienced growing demands on its public and private retirement systems. A later retirement age, however, does not at present appear to be one of the more seriously considered responses to those demands.

Such a step would seem to run counter to a prevailing attitude that early retirement is a social achievement, or that early retirement works to the public good because it (presumably) frees up jobs for younger workers. In Sweden, for instance, retirement age was lowered from 67 to 65 as recently as 1976. The government in France is lowering the highest retirement-age limits (high-ranking civil servants and full university professors). Strong pressure also exists to reduce retirement age for women in France.[5] Germany's flexible retirement age makes it increasingly easy for a worker to withdraw from the labor force at a relatively young age. According to one estimate, every second worker retires before age 63. In the United Kingdom, where the normal pensionable age is 65 for men and 60 for women, some pressure exists to equalize retirement ages by lowering that of men. The Danish government, in response to unemployment problems, not long ago provided early retirement incentives to workers at age 60.

Chapters 2–4 review recent and projected demographic developments in these countries, as well as labor force and retirement trends and projections, that may affect the ability and willingness of the working-age population to support older dependents over the next several decades. Most immediately affected by these developments is the social security system in the five countries. The social security financial problem and proposed solutions to that problem are considered in Chapters 5 and 6; the extent to which some of the growing support burden can be shifted from the public sector to the private sector is assessed in Chapter 7.

One proposed solution to the growing dependency burden involves prolonging the working life. Chapter 8 evaluates the pros and cons of this solution. Chapters 9 and 10 review, respectively, European approaches to the aging problem and attitudes about support of the aged. Retirement-age policy in the United States is the subject of Chapter 11. A summary of the extent to which a higher retirement age seems feasible is presented in Chapter 12.

2
Aging and the Aged Population in Europe

The populations of the five European countries, like that of the United States, have been aging. Actually, the proportion 65 and older is higher in each of these countries than it is in the United States (table 2.1), a development that reflects trends that have been evident for many decades. Even as early as 1900, sizable differences among some countries could be highlighted. At the turn of the century, for example, 8 percent of the populations of Sweden and France, but only 4 percent in the United States, was 65 or older. Over the past 30 years alone, the proportion 65-plus has increased markedly in the five European countries and the United States. This increase has been especially pronounced in Denmark, Germany, and Sweden (table 2.1).

DECLINING FERTILITY

These increases in the aged proportion of the population are primarily due to low fertility rates which, in each of the countries, currently fall below a replacement-rate level of 2.1. Whether fertility rates will remain so low is, as the European co-researchers and others emphasize, a great unknown.

Actuaries who prepared recent population projections for the United States Security Administration argue that an eventual increase in the fertility rate to 2.1 constitutes the most plausible fertility scenario (Bayo and Faber, 1980). This argument is based on the contention that current low rates of fertility have never before been experienced in the United States and are, furthermore, too low to ensure replacement of the population. While one might reasonably question whether couples make their family planning decisions with total fertility rates in mind, a similar perspective is voiced by the Commission of the European Communities:

> It seems impossible in our view to envisage age-specific fertility rates remaining at their present low levels. This would be equivalent to saying that real generations could have final family sizes as low as 1.4 or 1.5 children per woman, which has never been recorded in any country. (Commission of the European Communities, 1978b, p. 7)

6

Table 2.1. Percentage of the Population Aged 65 and Older, 1900–1979

	1900	1930	1950	1960	1970	1979	% Increase 1950–1979
Denmark	na	na	9	11	12	14	56
France	8	9	11	12	13	14	27
Germany (FR)	5	6	9	11	13	15	67
Sweden	8	9	10	12	14	16	60
United Kingdom	5	7	11	12	13	14	27
United States	4	6	8	9	10	11	38

SOURCE: 1900 and 1930 figures from Miegel, 1981; 1950–1970 figures from International Labour Office, 1977; 1979 figures from Population Reference Bureau, 1981, and country reports.

Thus, the commission uses higher fertility assumptions than those currently presented by its member countries, although below-replacement rates (a maximum of 2.0) are still assumed.

On the other hand, our European co-researchers, in general, envisage a continuation of lower replacement-level fertility rates. For instance, the Danish report, citing a fertility rate of 1.7 in 1977 and 1978, presents projections that assume an increase to 1.8 in four years, where it will remain until the year 2000. French projections also assume a 1.8 fertility rate, in their case through 2050. The Swedish report discusses projections based on three fertility assumptions (1.5, 1.8, and 2.1 as of 1985). What is presented as the main alternative, however, assumes an increase in Swedish fertility from 1.6 to 1.8 between 1977 and 1985. The report from the United Kingdom notes merely that high and low fertility variants are included in official forecasts, but these forecasts are not further discussed.

Fertility rates are obviously crucial because they determine the number of workers or potential workers available to support older and younger dependents; so, widely discrepant evaluations of the dimensions of the dependency burden will flow from population projections based on alternative fertility assumptions.

Although the reports from our co-researchers generally acknowledge the importance (and unpredictability) of fertility rates, they typically do not provide us with alternative population projections deriving from alternative fertility assumptions. Whether this omission reflects official emphasis on certain projections, the unavailability of alternatives, a desire not to overwhelm the reader with statistics, or some other factor, is unclear. The British report, however, reveals a clear skepticism of fertility assumptions, noting that the record of long- and even medium-term predictors of fertility in the United Kingdom indicates that they are "first cousins to astrology" and that absolute predictions cannot be made. Undoubtedly, most responsible demographers and actuaries would urge caution in interpreting population projections. Some reasonable range of alternatives, however, is generally regarded as necessary for responsible contingency planning.

The impact of alternative fertility assumptions is most apparent from the German report, which included projections to the year 2050 based on two assumptions of the net-reproduction rate (NRR). One assumption involved a continuation of the low 1976 rate of 0.66 and the other an increase in the NRR to 1.0 after 1991–2010.[1] An NRR of 1.0 would result in a stabilization of population size; a rate of less than 1.0 would contribute to a continued decline in population size.

Starting about the year 2000, the lower net-reproduction rate (0.66) would yield a slightly higher proportion of persons 60 and over than would the higher NRR (23.1 versus 22.8 percent). The differences would widen by about one percentage point every five years. By the year 2050, 22 percent of the German population would be 60 years old or over, if the NRR increases; if it does not, the "older" population—60-plus in the German projection—would comprise 31 percent of the population!

In the German case, the impact of alternative fertility assumptions is clear. Over the long run, a sharp increase in the aged-dependency ratio, as measured by population figures alone, would be evident if the net-reproduction rate does not begin to increase in the near future. According to the German report, this more pessimistic assumption is plausible because "it reflects an attitude on the part of the married couples which is satisfied, as a rule, by one or two children" (Eichner and Grossjohann, 1980, p. 22). A small family is seen as a response to work opportunities for women, family planning, and social attitudes. Since low reproduction rates have proven quite stable, any attitudinal change that would be reflected in higher birthrates would, in their words, take time. Consequently, Germany can expect a further decline in population, resulting from the small excess of deaths over births. By the year 2000, Germany's total population may have dropped from 56.8 million (1980) to around 52 million.

CHANGING AGE DISTRIBUTION

In view of recent developments in fertility rates, the below-replacement-rate fertility assumptions used in projections in the other country reports would appear to be the most reasonable assumptions. Even a dramatic increase in the fertility rate would have little impact on the aged-dependency ratio over the course of this century, although it would certainly increase the overall dependency ratio.[2] Through the first several decades of the next century, the smaller cohorts resulting from low fertility rates would be responsible for supporting the relatively large cohorts born in the 1950s and 1960s. Hence, these assumptions are, in the long run, more pessimistic than those generally accepted by policymakers in the United States. In any case, the end result is a steady decline in the proportion of young persons in these countries and a corresponding increase in the proportion of older persons.

In each of the five countries, population projections reveal a shift in the age distribution through and beyond the turn of the century. Barring any marked change in fertility, the population distributions of those countries should be consistent with the figures in table 2.2. With few exceptions, the general trends are similar across countries: a fairly sharp decline in the proportion of young (variously defined as 0–14 or 0–19) in the population by the end of the century, followed by a continued but less pronounced drop through the second decade of the twenty-first century. (Denmark, with a fairly consistent decline throughout this period, represents a slight deviation from this trend.) Each country will have experienced some increase in its aged population by the turn of the century. But in three of the five countries (Denmark, France, and Sweden), the increase over the next 20 years or so is relatively modest and much less pronounced than that which occurs after the

Table 2.2. Recent and Projected Age Distribution of the Population, Selected Years[1] (Percent)

	0–14	15–64	65+	% Inactive[2] and % Change
DENMARK[3]				
1977	21.6	64.3	14.2	35.8
2000	19.1	66.3	14.5	33.6
2020	17.1	64.7	18.2	35.3
% Change				
1977–2000	−11.6	+3.1	+2.1	−6.1
2000–2020	−10.5	−2.4	+25.5	+5.1
FRANCE[4]	0–19	20–24	65+	
1975	32.1	54.5	13.4	45.5
2000	26.0	59.5	14.5	40.5
2025	23.0	58.0	18.5	41.5
% Change				
1975–2000	−19.0	+9.2	+8.2	−11.0
2000–2025	−11.5	−1.7	+27.6	+2.5
GERMANY (FR)[5]	0–19	20–59	60+	
1977	26.5	52.6	20.9	47.4
2000	19.9	57.0	23.1	43.0
2020	16.3	56.8	26.9	43.2
% Change				
1977–2000	−24.9	+8.4	+10.5	−9.3
2000–2020	−18.1	−0.4	+16.4	+0.5
SWEDEN[6]	0–14	15–64	65+	
1977	20.4	63.9	15.7	36.1
2000	18.1	65.5	16.4	34.5
2025	16.8	63.1	20.0	36.8

Table 2.2 continued on p. 10

Table 2.2. (*continued*)

	0–14	15–64	65+	% Inactive[2] and % Change
% Change				
1977–2000	−11.3	+2.5	+4.5	−4.4
2000–2025	−7.2	−3.7	+22.0	+6.7
UNITED KINGDOM[7]	0–16	17–64	65+	
1977	24.0	61.5	14.5	38.5
1991	21.5	63.4	15.1	36.6
2001	23.3	62.4	14.3	37.6
% Change				
1977–1991	−10.4	+3.1	+4.1	−4.9
1991–2001	+8.4	−1.6	−5.3	+2.7
UNITED STATES[8]	0–19	20–64	65+	
1980	31.7	57.2	11.2	42.9
2000	28.0	58.8	13.2	41.2
2020	26.2	56.7	17.2	43.4
% Change				
1980–2000	−11.7	+2.8	+17.8	−4.0
2000–2020	−6.4	−3.6	+30.3	+5.3

SOURCE: Country reports; and Bayo and Faber, 1980.

[1] Comparable data across age groups and years were not available in the country reports.

[2] The sum of columns 1 and 3.

[3] Denmark: fertility assumption = 1.8 TFR; mortality = no change.

[4] France: fertility assumption = 1.8 TFR; mortality unspecified.

[5] Germany: net-reproduction rate of 0.66 since 1976; death rate varying until 1980.

[6] Sweden: fertility assumption = 1.8 TFR; mortality assumes relatively little change aside from a decline of (a) 1 percent/year for women over age 50 until 1985 and (b) 0.5 percent/year for men over 80, also until 1985.

[7] United Kingdom: assumptions unspecified.

[8] United States: fertility = ultimate TFR of 2.1 by 2005; for mortality, see Bayo and Faber (1980), Alternative II assumptions.

turn of the century, when a substantial increase in the pensionable population is expected as the high-fertility generations reach pensionable age.

Germany and the United Kingdom deviate from this pattern. In Germany, the increase in the older population should, if the assumptions underlying the projections are borne out, be much more consistent over the next 40 years or so: an 11 percent increase between 1977 and 2000 and a 16 percent increase between 2000 and 2020. In the United Kingdom, the proportion of elderly may be lower by the year 2000 than it was in 1977. After 2018, however, the aged proportion in the United Kingdom can be expected to increase, as persons born during the high birthrate period through the 1960s move to retirement age.

The potential significance of these changes will be discussed in Chapter 3. Nevertheless, it is worth pointing out that the relatively sanguine attitude that the European countries appear to have toward their aging populations is best expressed by the data in column 4 of table 2.2. In each of these countries, a decline in the percentage of persons of nonworking age is evident through the turn of the century. In other words, when numbers and proportions alone are considered, the declining youth population more than serves as an offset to the increasing older population. Moreover, in each country, a corresponding increase, albeit slight, in the population of "working age" also occurs over the near future. It is not until after the turn of the century that this apparently optimistic picture reverses itself.

THE "OLD OLD"

Over the short run, at least, these countries tend not to expect insurmountable problems in caring for their older populations, partly because of the belief that the cost of support will be offset to some extent by a decline in expenditures for young dependents. The 60- or 65-plus population, however, is anything but a homogeneous group, and the changing age distribution within the older population might be enough to dampen any complacency regarding the ability of the working-age population to support its older nonworkers without sizable tax increases. This indeed appears to be the case.

The United Kingdom report pinpoints the problem. It is expected that between 1977 and 2001, the number of persons above the present minimum pensionable age in that country will remain practically constant. Yet the very old—those 75 and older—will increase by 700,000, while the number of "young old" (74 or less) will drop by 800,000. The United Kingdom report emphasizes that the very old are heavy users of health services, residential homes, and other personal services. As a result of this increase in the very old segment of the population, the United Kingdom can expect "a net increase of £220–250 millions in current expenditure on health and personal services, plus capital expenditures to provide the necessary facilities" (Fogarty, 1980a, pp. 7–8).[3]

Data on the very old in these countries are not presented in a format that facilitates perfect comparability. Nevertheless, the available data do highlight an aging of the older populations (table 2.3). In Sweden, the 75-plus age group may be 44 percent larger by the turn of the century than it was in 1975; the 85-plus segment may almost double. In France, the 75-plus and 85-plus age groups will increase by 25 and 74 percent, respectively, while the total aged population (65-plus) will increase by only 16 percent. Denmark's population 75-plus currently comprises 39 percent of the population 65 and older; by the year 2000 that figure will reach 47 percent. All of these figures assume no significant mortality improvements.

Over the short run, Germany represents the most extreme example of an

Table 2.3. Recent and Projected Aged Distribution of the Older Population, Selected
Years (Percent)

	65–74	75–84	85+
DENMARK			
1979	61.4	31.4	7.2
1985	57.8	33.6	8.6
1990	56.0	34.5	9.6
1995	55.1	34.2	10.7
2000	52.9	35.4	11.6
FRANCE			
1975	62.3	30.6	7.1
2000	59.3	30.1	10.6
2025	59.4	31.7	8.9
GERMANY (FR)			
1975	66.9	33.1 (75+)	
1980	63.6	36.4 (75+)	
1990	45.2	54.7 (75+)	
SWEDEN			
1975	62.7	30.6	6.6
1980	60.6	32.0	7.4
1985	57.6	33.9	8.4
1990	55.7	34.7	9.6
1995	53.2	35.7	11.0
2000	50.8	37.2	12.0
UNITED KINDGOM			
1977	63.7	29.7	6.6
1986	58.4	33.8	7.8
1991	57.4	33.7	8.9
2001	54.7	34.7	10.6
UNITED STATES			
1980	60.5	29.5	10.0
1990	57.0	31.8	11.2
2000	51.0	34.2	14.7
2020	57.8	28.0	14.2

SOURCE: Country reports; and Bayo and Faber, 1980, Alternative II assumptions.

aging older population. The German report does not provide detailed age
breakdowns for any years after 1990. By that year, however, Germany's aged
population will be considerably "older" than any of the other countries in
this project: 55 percent will be 75 or older, in contrast to 44 percent in
Denmark and Sweden, 43 percent in the United Kingdom and the United
States, and perhaps 47 percent in France (the latter's figures are from the
Commission of the European Communities, 1978b). As a percentage of the
total population 60 and older, for which figures are available, the very old
component is projected to increase from 24 percent in 1975 to 33 percent in

1990, and then to drop to 27 percent in 2010. By 2020, their share of the aged population will have increased again—to 30 percent.

While this aging of the older population will, to some extent, be halted when the large "baby-boom" cohorts of the late 1940s, 1950s, and early 1960s reach retirement age, the immediate future promises an increase in expenditures for health care and supportive services for the growing population of "vulnerable" aged. All of the authors highlight this development as an area of concern in their respective countries.

INCREASING LONGEVITY

Mortality declines and improvements in life expectancy have also contributed to the increase in the *number* of older persons in each of these countries, although the impact of these developments on the age distribution and proportion of elderly has been negligible to date.

With the possible exception of the French, the prospect of future mortality declines in the upper ages does not appear to have generated much interest among the authors of the country reports. Each of the reports refers to, or includes statistics on, substantial increases in life expectancy that have occurred over the past several decades (table 2.4). These improvements have apparently continued well into the 1970s.

There is some tendency in the reports to stress that much (if not most) of this improvement is due to the decline in deaths from diseases that affect younger persons, rather than in those diseases and conditions responsible for death among the elderly. Few would quarrel with this observation. However, it is significant that improvement in life expectancy has also been evident at the upper ages as well (table 2.5). German data reveal improvements through age 90. In terms of years added to life expectancy, the gain at age 60 (or 70, 80, or 90) is obviously less spectacular than at birth. Even these "modest" improvements, however, may have significant consequences for the dependency burden, particularly if they manifest themselves over a relatively short period of time. At age 60, for example, French males had a life expectancy in 1977 that was one-half year longer than it was just two years previously. That is another half-year, on the average, that pension payments must be made. If such improvements had not been entered into pension-fund cost projections—and it is unlikely that they were—then this is another unanticipated demand on those pension funds.[4]

Opinions regarding further improvements in mortality are mixed at best. The authors of the Swedish report contend that mortality rates in the upper ages are now so low that large changes would be required to alter the age distribution, and, presumably, such an event is considered unlikely. The

Table 2.4. Life Expectancy at Birth, Selected Years

Approximate Year	Denmark		France		Germany		Sweden		United Kingdom	
	Men	Women	Men	Women	Men	Women	Men	Women	Men	Women
1900	52.9	56.2	45.0	48.5	44.8	48.3	55	57	48.1	51.8
1930	60.9	62.6	54.8	59.6	59.9	62.8	64	66	58.4	62.5
1950	67.8	70.1	63.4	69.2	64.6	68.5	71	74	66.2	71.2
1960	70.4	73.8	67.0	73.6	66.9	72.4	72	76	67.9	73.8
1970	70.7	75.9	68.4	75.8	67.4	73.8	72	77	68.9	75.1
1975	71.1	76.8	69.0	76.9	68.6	75.2	72.1	77.9	69.4	75.6
1977	71.5	77.5	69.7	77.8	na	na	na	na	na	na

SOURCE: Country reports; Keyfitz and Flieger, 1968; United Nations, *Demographic Yearbook*, 1972 and 1978.

Table 2.5. Life Expectancy at Age 60, Selected Years

Approximate Year	Denmark		France		Germany		Sweden		United Kingdom	
	Men	Women	Men	Women	Men	Women	Men	Women	Men	Women
1900	15.0	16.3	13.1	14.4	13.1	14.2	15.6	16.8	13.4	14.9
1930	15.9	16.3	13.6	15.9	15.1	16.1	16.6	17.4	14.4	16.4
1950	17.2	17.9	15.4	18.4	16.2	17.5	17.3	18.4	14.7	18.0
1960	17.3	19.0	15.7	19.5	15.5	18.5	17.5	19.5	15.0	19.0
1970	17.1	20.6	16.2	20.8	15.3	19.1	17.4	20.3	15.4	19.9
1975	17.1	21.1	16.5	21.3	15.8	19.9	17.6	21.4	15.5	20.1
1977	17.3	21.6	17.0	22.0	na	na	na	na	na	na

SOURCE: Country reports; Keyfitz and Flieger, 1968; United Nations, *Demographic Yearbook*, 1972 and 1978.

Swedes, in fact, note an actual increase in mortality among middle-aged men in recent years—the first such reported increase aside from catastrophic events (such as war). Should this increase be sustained or appear among women and other age groups, then projections of the older population might overestimate future dependency burdens. The Swedish co-researchers seem to be anything but optimistic about developments in mortality, at least in the short run. In contrast, they postulate that should death rates from any one disease decline, the death rate from other diseases would increase because of a tendency for weaknesses in several organs to coexist in old age. The German report likewise pays scant attention to the issue of mortality improvements, because of a belief that "even severe changes would not have great effects on the total population in the very near future (Eichner and Grossjohann, 1980, p. 27). As far as percentages are concerned, this observation is undoubtedly correct. *Numbers*, however, and expenditures, can be affected by less dramatic improvements.

If the British argument is accepted, any further improvements in mortality and life expectancy depend largely on modifications in life-style—changes that are believed to be beyond the control of government. A similar argument is raised in the Swedish report, which maintains that the government has more control over collective than individual actions. The Swedish report maintains that "one further reason for being skeptical as regards possibilities to obtain a fall in mortality rates is that it requires influencing individuals directly" (Berglind and Bergroth, 1980, p. 20).

With the exception of the French, none of the co-researchers places much stock in any biomedical development or technological breakthrough that may result in any marked lengthening of the life span. A supplement to the United Kingdom report that deals with mortality projections contends that projections of life prolongation are too speculative for the basis of practical mortality projections (Benjamin and Overton, 1980), an opinion that appears to underlie discussions in the Danish, German, and Swedish reports. This is also the case in the United States.

The Germans, as noted above, did evaluate the impact of two divergent fertility assumptions in the age distribution of the population. It was assumed, however, that mortality rates would remain relatively stable. The Danes contend that mortality trends clearly indicate a shift in the direction of relatively more aged, but the authors are doubtful whether any breakthroughs in all age groups will manifest themselves.

Official Swedish statistics assume that mortality rates will, on the whole, remain at recent levels. They do, however, assume that for women over 50 and for men over 80, mortality rates will decline by 1.0 and 0.5 percent, respectively, each year until 1985. Aside from a minor decline for women 60 and older during 1979 and 1980 only, the Danish population projections also assume that mortality will remain unchanged, resulting in only a slightly higher number of aged persons. Only the French suggest that projections of eight million aged by the twenty-first century, as opposed to the present seven million, are likely to be underestimates because of the "very conservative" mortality assumptions used in those projections. The report makes the very significant observation that as of 1977, life expectancy at birth had already reached the level that previous projections had set for the year 2000.

Alternative population projections based on a range of mortality assumptions are available only in the supplement to the United Kingdom report that dealt with prospects for mortality decline (Benjamin and Overton, 1980). The text of this report leaves the reader with the strong impression that the authors anticipate very little in the way of substantial mortality declines. Nevertheless, in their three projections, they assume either of the following:

1. A continuation of current trends in age-specific death rates for each sex
2. No improvement in mortality over age 30
3. Elimination of most cancers and a postponement by 10 years of death from most diseases

The pessimistic projection (2) would yield a pensionable-age population comprising 18.8 percent of the population in 2017, as compared to 17.9 percent in 1979. Under the most optimistic projection (3), 27 percent of the population would be above pension age, while what might be termed the conservative, or middle-of-the-road, projection results in a figure of 21.3 percent of the population above pension age. Depending on the development considered most probable, marked increases in demands on pension funds and support services would be expected and, presumably, planned for. In this case, the optimistic scenario is apparently regarded as the least likely development (and indeed, the assumptions underlying it are rather extreme). The more conservative improvement increases the proportion of pensioners by fewer than 4 percentage points over the 1979 figure and may, over the next 40 years, be easily accommodated.

The French report is the only European one that acknowledges a fairly good possibility of substantial mortality improvements and carries these improvements through in population projections. In the French case, the hypothetical improvements fall far short of a biomedical breakthrough. They represent, instead, areas well within the realm of improvement, given current medical knowledge. They assume, for example, improvements resulting from fewer high-risk jobs, a narrowing of differences between men and women in social behavior (for example, in employment, consumption, and leisure), vigorous campaigns against alcoholism, and more attention to physical condition. Under this scenario, life expectancy at birth would increase to age 79 for women and 73 for men. Translated into persons, 8.9 million persons in France would be 65 or older in the year 2000, up from 8.1 million for that year under the more conservative assumptions. A 10 percent increase in the elderly population is no minor event.

As with fertility assumptions, only the future will prove how far-sighted or myopic these assumptions about mortality are. Whether past assumptions about mortality in these countries have turned out to be accurate is impossible to ascertain from the available data. Only the French co-researchers cite the inadequacy of previous population projections in light of unexpected mortality declines.

In the United States, official underestimates of mortality improvements at the upper ages have been the subject of considerable criticism. More recent projections, particularly those of the Social Security Administration, now provide a wider range of mortality assumptions that may enable policymakers to anticipate better the magnitude of the aged support burden should mortality rates at the upper ages continue to decline. The differences are striking. For the year 2000, conservative mortality assumptions result in a projection of 34.4 million persons 65 and older. Under the middle-range assumptions, approximately 36 million Americans would fall into this age group, while the "optimistic" alternative projects some 39 million aged. Depending on the mortality assumptions, the population 95 and older may be anywhere from 222 to 527 percent larger by the turn of the century than it was in 1980.

At the very least, it seems reasonable to suggest that life expectancy in Denmark, France, Germany, and the United Kingdom will approach that of Sweden, or that life expectancy of males in each of these countries will approach that of females. Should that occur, or should the improvements be even more dramatic, then these countries will find themselves with an increasing number of persons outliving their projected life expectancy. Unless compensated for by an increase in fertility rates or in labor-force participation or a much healthier economy, already strained pension funds and other support systems may be ill-equipped to meet the additional, unexpected demands placed upon them.

3

A Crisis in Support?

THE DEPENDENT POPULATION

The impact of the changing age distribution in these countries is most graphically and conveniently depicted in the dependency ratio, which is merely a ratio of nonworkers in a population to workers (or, more commonly, persons of working age). The easiest method of computing dependency ratios is to use age alone in defining persons as supporters or dependents. Although not very sophisticated measures, age-specific dependency ratios serve as meaningful indicators of the impact of demographic developments on the supporters in a population.

In conventional dependency ratios in the United States, supporters typically include everyone between the ages of 16 or, more recently, 19 and 65. The remaining segments of the population constitute the dependents. Some retirement experts have argued that if age is to remain the sole determinant of dependency status, 62 might be regarded as the more appropriate entry point into old age, since a majority of older workers now opt to collect actuarially reduced retirement benefits before age 65. Projections in government and other policy documents (such as the Social Security Trustees and Advisory Committee reports) nonetheless are still based on the assumption that aged dependency begins at 65.

Each of the European researchers addressed the issue of changing dependency ratios, although, as with many of the issues, the emphasis placed on dependency ratios varied across reports, as did the specificity of statistics. The United Kingdom report, for example, simply notes that the active (working-age) population will increase from 47.9 percent of the total population to 50.8 by 1991, thus reducing somewhat the *overall* burden of support. Nevertheless, it was possible from the country reports and supplemental data to extract or compute dependency ratios for each country at least through the turn of the century.

The age distributions in table 2.2 imply that support burdens will probably be manageable in most of these countries over the next 10 or 20 years, given the increased proportion of persons of working age in these countries. This observation tends to be supported by the dependency ratios themselves, as column 3 in table 3.1 indicates.[1] In each country, the total dependency

Table 3.1. Estimates and Projections of Age-Specific Dependency Ratios,[1] Selected Years

	Dependency Ratio			Aged as Percent of Dependent Population
	Youth	Aged	Total	
DENMARK[2]				
1979	34	22	56	39
2000	29	22	51	43
2010	26	23	49	47
2020	26	28	54	52
2030	27	31	58	53
FRANCE[3]				
1975	59	25	84	30
2000	44	24	68	35
2025	39	32	71	45
GERMANY (FR)[4]				
1977	50	40	90	44
1980	45	37	82	45
1990	32	35	67	51
2000	35	40	75	53
2010	30	42	72	58
2020	29	47	76	62
2030	32	66	98	67
SWEDEN[5]				
1977	32	25	57	44
2000	28	25	53	47
2025	27	32	58	55
UNITED KINGDOM[6]				
1977	41	29	70	41
1991	35	29	64	45
2001	39	27	66	41
UNITED STATES[7]				
1980	55	20	75	27
1990	49	22	70	31
2000	48	22	70	31
2020	46	30	76	39

SOURCE: Country reports; and Bayo and Faber, 1980.

[1] Number of dependents per 100 persons of "working age."

[2] Denmark: youth = 0–14; aged = 65+; fertility assumption = 1.8 TFR; mortality, no change.

[3] France: youth = 0–19; aged = 65+; fertility assumption = 1.8 TFR; mortality unspecified.

[4] Germany: youth = 0–19; aged = 60+; net reproduction of 0.66 since 1976; death rate varying until 1980.

[5] Sweden: youth = 0–14; aged = 65+; fertility assumption = 1.8 TFR; mortality assumes relatively little change aside from a decline of (a) 1 percent/year for women over age 50 until 1985 and (b) 0.5 percent/year for men over 80, also until 1985.

[6] United Kingdom: youth = 0–15; aged = 60+ for women and 65+ for men; assumptions unspecified.

[7] United States: youth = 0–19; aged = 65+; fertility assumption = ultimate TFR of 2.1 by 2005; for mortality, see Bayo and Faber (1980), Alternative II assumptions.

burden declines, often sharply, at least through 1990 or 2000. In Denmark, a continuation of this decline is projected through 2010.

The improvement in the dependency ratio is due almost exclusively to the decline in young persons as a percentage of the total population. Changes in the aged dependency ratio are, with the exception of Germany, almost non-existent through the turn of the century.

Demographic developments and their effects are likely to be most extreme in Germany, where the population is actually shrinking. In that country, the total dependency ratio is expected to drop sharply between 1977 and 1990—from 90 to 67 dependents per 100 persons of working age, a decline of 23 dependents or 26 percent. Most, but not all, of this decline results from the assumed very low birthrates (accounting for 18 of those dependents). The aged dependency ratio, however, also declines, as the small birth cohorts from the 1930s reach their sixties. After 1990 or so, the total dependency ratio should begin to inch upward, drop again for a period of years, and then begin a steep climb. However, barring any marked changes in fertility or mortality, the total dependency ratio in Germany may not approach its 1977 level until *after* 2020.

Although the total dependency ratio shows little deterioration over the next half-century or so, the composition of the dependent population will undergo dramatic changes in Germany. In 1977, about two-fifths of all the dependents were "old" dependents (60-plus). By 2010, almost three-fifths of the dependent population will consist of older persons, and by 2020, almost two-thirds. The significance of these statistics lies in the fact that the changing age composition of a dependent population may make a big difference when it comes to costs.

The trends appear to be roughly similar in the other European countries, as table 3.1 highlights. The youth dependency ratio declines fairly steadily, with the exception of the United Kingdom—where a slight increase is projected between 1991 and 2001. In no country is an increase in the aged dependency ratio apparent until almost the turn of the century at the earliest. After the turn of the century, the aged dependency ratio begins to climb well above its mid-to-late-1970s level in Denmark, France, Sweden, and West Germany. (In the United Kingdom, projections were carried through only to 2001.) At the same time, everything else being equal, the total dependency ratio will also increase. In France however, the total dependency ratio for the year 2025 remains well below its 1975 level, while in Sweden and Denmark, the projected increase as of 2025 and 2030, respectively, results in a total dependency ratio that is only slightly larger than it was in the late 1970s.

Despite these rather optimistic ratios (youth, aged, and total) evident over the short run, it is significant that the composition of the dependent populations does not remain stable in any one of these countries. They become increasingly older, with the possible exception of the United Kingdom, where the percentage of old in the dependent population increases to 1991 and then decreases. (Projections from the EEC reveal an eventual increase in the United Kingdom as well.) It is possible that other countries will experience comparable dips in intervening years; however, population projections in the country reports generally encompassed very broad time spans. Any such dips, if they exist, have been obscured and are probably insignificant in view of the overall trend toward increasingly *aged* dependent populations in Denmark, France, Germany, and Sweden (column 4 of table 3.1).

THE YOUTH OFFSET

Given that the total dependency ratio typically improves over the next 10 or 20 years, but that an increasing percentage of those dependents is of pensionable age, the relative costs of supporting young and old dependents becomes the crucial issue. Will declining costs for the smaller percentage of young dependents serve as an offset to the growing costs for older ones? And if so, to what extent? Or will the body politic decide to spend the savings that result from a reduction in the ratio of dependent young to total population on improved benefits for the young?

As of 1975 in the United States, it was estimated that public expenditures for older dependents (65-plus) were about three times as great as those for young (0–17) dependents: $3,271 versus $1,215 (Clark, 1976). The expenditures themselves have obviously increased since 1975, but should the ratio remain stable, the aging of the dependent population would ensure an increase in the total dependency burden over the long run. In other words, no dollar-for-dollar offset can be expected as the ratio of young to old shifts over coming decades.

Over the short term, however, the burden would decline. As a percentage of disposable income, these cost projections by Robert Clark reveal a steady drop in the total dependency burden after 1990 and through 2010 (table 3.2). During this period (1990–2010), the youth dependency burden declines; the

Table 3.2. Public Costs of Supporting Dependents as a Percentage of Disposable Personal Income, United States 1975–2020[1]

Dependents	1975	1990	2000	2010	2020
Youth	7.49	6.66	6.53	6.07	6.08
Aged	7.74	8.71	8.60	8.80	10.74
Total	15.23	15.37	15.13	14.87	16.82

SOURCE: Robert Clark, cited in Sheppard and Rix, *The Graying of Working America*, 1977, Table 5. Reprinted by permission of The Free Press.
[1] Assumes constant relative expenditures and replacement-level fertility.

aged burden also declines for a period of time. After the baby-boom cohorts reach retirement age, total and aged dependency costs rise sharply.

The dependent cost projections by Clark are actually likely to underestimate the eventual differential in expenditures for young and old dependents, since his analyses did not take into account the aging of the older population and a corresponding increase in support costs. It is, of course, possible that the youth burden will also rise. A fertility increase would foster such a development, as would pressures for greater public expenditures for youth, such as expanded training programs, public day-care facilities, or improvements in educational institutions.

Available European data also paint, for the most part, a rather optimistic picture for the next few years. *Public* expenditures for persons of pensionable age in the United Kingdom, for example, are reported to be double those of children of compulsory school age and triple those of younger children. According to the United Kingdom report, no change in this ratio is expected. If correct, the declining youth population in the United Kingdom is expected to produce some offset to the increasing older population through the turn of the century, assuming continuation of current rates of expenditures. The United Kingdom report did note, on the other hand, a concern with rising expenditures for the very old. Whether this development was considered in the offset calculations is not clear; however, the report does conclude that demographic trends up to the turn of the century "are likely to ease rather than aggravate the problem of support for the elderly." (Fogarty, 1980a, p. 15).

The French co-researchers take a different approach to evaluating the potential offset factor. Their calculations assume, for example, that the cost of an inactive youth in France is one-half that of an adult aged 25–59. The cost of an aged person, 60-plus, is reported to be only slightly higher: 60 percent. Applying these percentages to the population distribution for 1975, 2000, 2025, and 2040, they obtain a "load coefficient" that reveals a decline in the support burden through the year 2000, after which it begins to pick up. Assuming a stabilization of those expenditure percents—which is a fairly big assumption—the load coefficient, or support burden, drops from .55 in 1975 to .45 in 2000. By 2040, the load coefficient is expected to increase to .54, still below the 1975 figure.

Unfortunately, it is not clear whether these figures include private (such as familial) expenses for the care of dependents, or refer only to public expenditures—a significant point, as we discuss below. Thus, any conclusions of offsets must be tempered with that observation in mind. The above figures suggest that the declining youth population would more than offset the cost of supporting the aging population in France well into the next century. However, there is no guarantee, as Paillat points out, that the declining number of young will automatically allow the transfer of resources to the growing aged population.[2] This is a very important point.

A similar conclusion is reached by the Danish co-researchers, who—with many caveats (including an assumption that the relative public expenditures for young and old dependents will not change)—estimate future support costs as a percentage of GNP. These are presented in table 3.3.

In 1979 public expenditures for an aged person in Denmark were more than double those for a young dependent (Kr 55,900 versus Kr 24,600). If these average amounts remain stable, and if population and GNP projections are borne out,[3] then reduced expenditures for the young may "more than counteract" any increase in expenditures for the aged (Friis and Hansen, 1980). As table 3.3 highlights, the elderly would account for a growing proportion of the burden, but that burden undergoes relatively little change for some 30 years. After 2010, however, the offset is no longer evident. The youth "burden" continues to decline, while the aged burden and total burden undergo pronounced increases (of 26 and 13 percent, respectively, between 2010 and 2030).

The German report also tackles the offset issue in some detail. Research in Germany indicates that total public and private support costs for a young person to age 20 are one-third higher than those for an older person from age 60 to the end of his or her life. Thus, at least over the next 15 to 20 years, "the rising amount of old-age benefits . . . will presumably be offset by reductions in dependency costs which at present are not covered by social benefits," for example, support, education, and training of the young (Eichner and Grossjohann, 1980, p. 56).[4]

An important point, however, is that the reductions in youth expenditures generally affect public *and* family budgets, while insured workers carry the public costs of increasing social security benefits for the aged (Eichner and Grossjohann, 1980). Increasing social security benefits are more readily identified and measured than family expenditures for children. This fact high-

Table 3.3. Dependency Burden as Percent of GNP, Denmark 1979–2030[1]

Year	Youth	Aged	Total	Aged as % of Total
1979	11.2	12.7	23.9	53
2000	10.0	13.2	23.2	57
2010	9.3	14.0	23.3	60
2030	8.3	17.6	26.4	67

SOURCE: Friis and Hansen, 1980.
[1] Public expenditure, based on amount per person in 1979.

lights one of the weaknesses associated with attempts to evaluate the relative magnitudes of dependency burdens.

Needless to say, much of the burden of child care falls squarely on the shoulders of family breadwinners. Just how great that burden is—and, indeed, if it is perceived as a burden—depends on factors that may vary widely across families (such as number of children, number of employed adults, and social values). Espenshade (1980) estimates that it costs some $85,000 for a middle-class family to raise a child to age 18 in the United States. Families may cope with rising costs by having fewer children, saving less, working more, reducing expenditures for other things, or any of a variety of ways. Whatever families spend themselves is perhaps less important than the fact that reliance on public expenditures may provide a misleading perception of future dependency burdens.[5] More comprehensive and better data on the costs of various dependents are clearly warranted.

Concern about the aged dependency ratio may arise and may be perceived as a burden because, as Wander (1978, p. 57) points out, "the respective individual contributions are clearly identified on the wage bill." The same is not true for young dependents who may indeed, if the German data are any more precise, be a greater economic burden.

Moreover, more than costs are involved in the youth-offset issue. The plausibility of the "youth-offset" argument would be increased if the resources released as a result of a decrease in children were reallocated through an automatic market mechanism. But this mechanism does not operate in such a case. As Bruno Stein puts it, "even though the resources may be available, their transfer from the young to the old becomes a political rather than an economic issue" (Stein, 1980, p. 204).

Creating mechanisms of transfer is not so "simple" as enacting a piece of federal legislation. Youth educational expenditures, for instance, constitute one area where savings from a declining birthrate might be realized. School budgets, however, are under local jurisdictions, of which there are thousands in the United States. The effort involved in encouraging those local jurisdictions to transfer any school savings to programs for the elderly would be overwhelming, the cost of which could far exceed the possible benefits. Furthermore, there is scant evidence to support a contention that communities would favor such transfers; they might prefer to improve existing school systems or use the money for any of dozens of other purposes.

Similar arguments can be raised to counter the suggestion that the smaller families of the present might be able to pay more in taxes to meet the support demands of a growing retired population. This suggestion implies that fewer children leave greater resources to spend on something or someone else. The increase in the cost of raising children (Espenshade, 1977 and 1980) raises questions about the validity of such suggestions. It is quite possible that the expense of raising children has contributed to the decision to limit family size. In addition, parents themselves just might prefer investing more in those fewer children—or perhaps their own parents—to supporting the anonymous elderly population.

ADDITIONAL CONCERNS

As shown in the preceding discussion on the relationship between population dependency ratios and the cost burden, the crude dependency ratio may not be the most appropriate measure of dependency burdens. Several of the reports suggest that, despite more favorable dependency ratios, the burden to the working or taxpaying public will increase long before the dependency ratio (aged or total) begins its upward climb. The maturation of various pension funds, past liberalization of promised benefits, expansion of social and health services to the elderly, and lower retirement ages are but a few of the factors contributing to the taxpayer's burden.

The French report notes, for example, that the financial burden of supporting the aged has increased by 75 percent since 1954, not only because of demographic and economic trends, but also as a result of a policy of giving more money to the aged, whose standard of living was very low in the 1950s and 1960s. Old-age expenditures increased by a factor of 6 in France between 1966 and 1978. Credits for the elderly increased 1.5 times more than salaries. Between 1970 and 1977, the ratio of beneficiaries to contributors in the French general (pension) scheme rose from 0.26:1 to 0.35:1.

Although the picture in Germany looks fairly rosy, the long-range consequences of the changing age distribution, judging from dependency ratios, are less optimistic. Scientists on the Advisory Council to the Ministry of Economic Affairs in Germany have developed two models to ascertain the magnitude of the dependency burden by 2030 under two divergent conditions. In simplified form, the first model assumes that the level of benefits to the elderly will remain reasonably stable throughout this period. The contribution rate then changes to accomodate the increase in the aged population. In the second model, contribution rates remain the same, but pension size and costs decrease to adapt to a stable contribution rate.[6]

Under the first model (stable benefit levels), contribution rates will rise from the 1980 level of 18 percent of gross income to 32.5 percent, an increase of 80 percent. If health insurance and unemployment insurance contributions are added to those for social security, employers and employees would be making contributions that amount to 40 percent of wages. To this must be added direct taxes for the employee, which means that payroll deductions for an average income would exceed 50 percent by 2030.

Under the second model (stable contribution rates), benefit levels can only fall. Instead of the present average gross income-replacement rate of 46 percent, only about 25 to 27 percent of gross income would be replaced under the reduction necessary to ensure a stable contribution rate.

Quite likely, the consequences evolving from either main condition in the two models (stable benefit rates or stable contributions) would arouse substantial opposition from one group or another—workers who might be faced with a substantially higher tax burden under model 1, or retirees, whose replacement rate would be considerably reduced under model 2.

The German scientists who developed the models conclude that in both cases, economically and socially undesirable results would accompany a reduction in population over the long run (2030 and later). In their opinion, a tax burden of more than 50 percent (model 1) "is likely to impair seriously the willingness to work of the age groups which are expected to enter and stay in the labor force" (in Eichner and Grossjohann, 1980, pp. 60–61). This, in turn, would "not only impede the development of productivity . . . but would also lead to social tensions." Freezing real pension income at the 1980 level would, aside from the social problems associated with a sharply reduced income, most probably force more older persons to work. The advisory council opposes prolonged labor force participation that is brought about by economic duress.

By the turn of the century in Denmark, according to Friis and Hansen, expenditures for the elderly as a percent of GNP should be only 1.4 percent higher than the 1979 level, assuming the underlying assumptions are borne out. This would be, they note, tantamount to an extra spending of Kr 5 billion at 1979 prices. Compared to present taxation pressures, consisting of personal taxes and duties that amounted to 45 percent of GNP, an increase of 1.4 percent may indeed appear modest.

THE DEPENDENCY BURDEN AND RETIREMENT AGE

From these reports, one gathers that the European countries[7] are not faced with an insurmountable support burden any time soon. Therefore, convincing the public that there is a potential support-burden crisis when the total and aged dependency ratios are declining would appear to be a rather futile undertaking, especially in those countries where decreasing expenditures for young dependents may offset any increase for aged dependents. A proposal to raise retirement age seems particularly improbable in view of high unemployment in many of these countries,[8] productivity declines in at least some of them, and the increasing demand for jobs on the part of the relatively large cohorts of younger workers and women seeking to enter or reenter the labor force. The Swedish report sums up the situation most explicitly: at the present time "there is a relatively limited interest [in giving] the elderly over age 65 a stronger position in the labor market" (Berglind and Bergroth, 1980, p. 38).

In the United States, on the other hand, acknowledgment of the eventuality of a higher retirement age is becoming more widespread. Like those in the five European countries, trends in the overall U.S. dependency ratio provide little grounds for alarm until after the year 2010 or so when the baby-boom cohorts reach what is currently the normal retirement age. The impact of early retirement, high inflation, and unemployment has, however, hardly gone unnoticed as a result of highly publicized concern about the solvency of the social security system.

The financial status of the social security trust funds has been subjected to increasing public scrutiny in recent years; the general consensus is that social security, given prevailing retirement trends and the very sizable improvement in mortality at the upper ages, will not be able to meet its promised benefit commitments from payroll taxes in 20 years or so. In fact, interfund borrowing has already become necessary. Raising retirement age, as discussed in Chapter 11, has been recommended as one way to alleviate the demands on social security. A higher retirement age is not the only possible solution to this "crisis" in the United States; higher payroll taxes, financing through general revenues, and reduced benefits have also been proposed. Still, a gradual rise in retirement age from 65 to 68 over the next two or three decades seems an increasingly likely prospect. However, there is no evidence that the five European countries are moving in this direction.

From all accounts, a higher retirement age is not being seriously debated in official circles in any of the five European countries examined in this book. If anything, interest has centered on a lower retirement age—for example, the push to lower to age 60 the pensionable age for men in the United Kingdom, the 1976 reduction in retirement age in Sweden, and the introduction of more flexible retirement limits in Germany.

To the extent that inflation, liberalization of benefit levels to retirees, and expanded health and social services resulting from the aging of the older population are reflected in increased taxes carried by the worker and other taxpayers, some resentment and demand for relief may manifest themselves. It is doubtful, however, whether a higher retirement age will be considered a serious policy option in any of these countries in the foreseeable future. None of the reports, for example, estimated the benefit reductions that might accrue from a higher retirement age, perhaps because this development presently appears, at best, to be but a remote possibility.

In *Retirement-Age and Retirement Costs: The Long-Term Challenge*, Fogarty (1980b) warns that, although delayed retirement may result in some gain in tax and contribution payments, persons who postpone retirement are also likely to be earning increased pension entitlements. He discusses a proposal for the United Kingdom whereby social security and occupational pensions would, except for the physically and mentally disabled, be payable at half-rate up to age 70. As a rough estimate of the savings, Fogarty notes that at a half-rate up to age 69, National Insurance pension payments in 1978/1979 would have reduced expenditures by £1.5 billion. Another £450 billion would have been saved if the same rule had applied to occupational pensions. Work opportunities would have to be available, "but the size of the resources which it could release for the benefit, in particular, of more elderly or disabled pensioners make it worth considering as and when these conditions have been considered" (Fogarty, 1980b, p. 148).

There is also, of course, the sobering fact that a smaller youth population becomes a smaller working-age population that must be relied upon to support a much larger and growing nonworking older population. The ability of this population to provide adequate support obviously depends on more than numbers of people. Wander (1978, p. 55) points out that the transition to zero population growth "has never led to an economic setback or breakdown of pension systems, as was prophesied by many observers whenever birth rates turned down." In the case of Germany, which is analyzed in some detail, an increase in the share of workers' income to pension funds did occur between 1920 and 1975, but rapid economic expansion meant no reduction in standard of living. Whether this will hold true in the future is a big question to be discussed subsequently.

These countries are not unconcerned about rising public expenditures for the elderly. Nor are they unconcerned about the potential burden to the taxpayer. It is merely that policy options other than a higher retirement age will be considered—and probably implemented—before the age at retirement is officially increased.

4

Trends in Work and Retirement

The crucial element in the dependency ratio is the number of nonworkers relative to the number employed or, more specifically, relative to the number of insured workers who contribute to retirement income systems.[1] Because some persons do not work in covered employment, the insured population is always smaller than the labor force population[2] which, in turn, is considerably smaller than the population of working age. The most precise definition of direct supporters includes only the insured, employed population. When such data are unavailable (which was the case in most country reports), labor-force participation rates serve as the most convenient proxy.

The age at which a worker may retire with full benefits varies somewhat across countries, as table 4.1 indicates. Denmark maintains the highest age of eligibility for full pension benefits (67 for males and married females), followed by France, Germany, Sweden, and the United States at 65 for both sexes. In the United Kingdom, females may retire at age 60, while males must wait until 65 for full pension benefits. Each European country permits earlier retirement under certain conditions, such as after a period of unemployment. In the United States, any worker who has contributed to the social security system for a minimum set number of quarters may receive actuarially reduced benefits at age 62.

"AVERAGE" RETIREMENT AGE

Only the German report provides information on average retirement age, and only for one year: in 1976, insured males and females who received their first pension (disregarding survivor benefits) were, on the average, 60.3 years old. The French state ony that there has been a significant lowering of age at retirement. The Swedish co-researchers also note that there is a growing number of persons who retire before the "normal" retirement age. The United Kingdom paper cites "an unmistakable downward trend" in the number of men who opt to work beyond age 65, especially those with decent pensions. In Denmark, on the other hand, prior to the introduction of the severance pay scheme[3] in January 1979, the average retirement age of wage and salary workers approached 67. Retirement tended to occur later among upper-level employees (closer to 70) and employees in the public sector.

Table 4.1. Retirement Age

Country	"Normal" Retirement Age	Minimum Retirement Age
Denmark	67 men and married women; 62 single women	60: severance benefit for members of unemployment funds; 55 adverse social and and employment-related circumstances; 60: handicapped
France	65 (60 with inadequate pensions)	60: premature (unemployment) pension, reducing until retirement pension due; also for work under difficult conditions
Germany (FR)	65	60 if unemployed for more than one year in the last year and one-half before age 60 or if handicapped and severely disabled with 35 years of coverage; 63 with 35 years of coverage; 60 for severely disabled women with 15 years of coverage and more than 120 contributions in the last 20 years
United Kingdom	65 men; 60 women	60 under job release options (originally 62 for men and 59 for women) if replaced by registered unemployed
United States	65	62 for actuarially reduced pension

Since the beginning of the 1960s, the decrease in retirement age has been sharpest among unskilled workers.

While these data are scanty, average retirement age is probably not all that meaningful a statistic. What matters is the number of older dependents; and the data from the five European countries indicate that labor force participation on the part of the elderly and even among the late middle-aged, particularly males, has been declining in most of them.

Because the format in which labor-force and/or contributor/beneficiary data are presented and detailed differs greatly among the country reports, comparisons across countries were not feasible. The following sections summarize, country by country, the relevant data on labor-force trends and projections.

Sweden

In many respects, Swedish trends in labor-force participation since the mid-1960s have been very similar to those in the United States. The participation rate among younger men (16–44) has remained virtually unchanged in both countries, while rates for older men (65–74) and even those in their middle years have dropped sharply. Between 1965 and 1978, for example, the employment rate among men 65–74 fell from 37 to 14 percent, while that among men between the ages of 45 and 64 dropped from 93 to 86 percent (see table 4.2 for employment rates). In Sweden, a substantial overall decrease in full-

Table 4.2. Employment Rates for Men and Women 16–74 Years Old, Sweden, 1965 and 1978

Sex and	PERCENT		% Change
Age	1965	1978	1965–1978
Men:			
16–24	70	70	—
25–44	97	96	−1.0
45–64	93	86	−7.5
65–74	37	14	−62.2
Women:			
16–24	60	68	+13.3
25–44	55	80	+45.4
45–64	49	67	+36.7
65–74	11	4	−63.6

SOURCE: Berglind and Bergroth, 1980.

time employment among middle-aged men has also been observed. Swedish women (and their counterparts in the United States) have manifested a marked increase in labor-force attachment at all ages except the oldest (65-plus).

The official short-term forecast in Sweden projects favorable developments through 1983, at least in terms of the *number* of persons employed in that country. Some 232,000 additional persons, largely women, are expected to be added to the labor force by 1983. These projections forecast a continued decline in the labor-force participation rates of men 45 and older.

Experts in Sweden, however, are not in agreement regarding the development of female employment. The Committee on Employment, for example, believes that halving the projected rate of increase among women would be more reasonable. In its defense, the committee argues that the projected increase presupposes strong labor-market pressures to get women into the labor force, as well as the availability of social services (such as child care) to facilitate employment.

Over the medium term (through the year 2000), the Swedish employment rate, calculated as the number of employed persons, is expected to increase under each of three alternative projection paths discussed in the report.[4] Not until the turn of the century is a decline in the number of employed projected. The size of that decline obviously depends on the underlying fertility assumption. In the most pessimistic scenario (fertility rate of 1.5), the Swedish labor force in 2025 may be 8 percent smaller than it was in the mid- to late 1970s. But that is not until after the turn of the century. Until then, the Swedish co-researchers apparently anticipate little interest in prolonging work life in that country. Instead, as the Committee on Employment points out, the need during the late 1980s and early 1990s will be for employment policies that "to an ever increasing extent [are] directed toward solving the

problems of the groups approaching age 50 and coming closer to the risk
zone for being 'eliminated' " (Berglind and Bergroth, 1980, p. 17). Similar
policies may be necessary in Denmark and the United States, since the labor
forces are middle-aging as the large cohorts of the 1940s and 1950s, respectively, reach their middle years.

Germany

In Germany, too, the labor-force participation rate of older males has been
declining for many years, a process facilitated by the introduction of flexible
retirement age and enhanced financial security in retirement. These developments have been hailed as social achievements, and as such, it would
appear that any modification of these advances would meet strong opposition. On the other hand, the possibility of a general reduction in retirement
age to age 60 has been raised by the Deutsche Gewerkschaftsbund (DGB) as
a means of reducing and preventing unemployment, but such a reduction
seems unlikely at this time.

The result of the retirement and labor-force policies and trends in Germany has been a substantial deterioration of the ratio of pension beneficiaries to employed contributors to the pension schemes in that country. Between 1960 and 1976, the ratio of annuitants to blue- and white-collar insured
workers increased from 0.374:1 to 0.559:1. This deterioration has been most
pronounced in the compulsory insurance system covering blue-collar workers, where the number of contributors has decreased by 11 percent since 1960
and the number of beneficiaries has increased by almost 60 percent. Through
the 1980s, however, these beneficiary/contributor ratios are expected to improve. Consequently, unless the tax burden increases as a result, say, of
liberalization of pension benefits or expanded social services for the very old,
pressures to raise retirement age are likely to be muted.

Unemployment rates that, by German standards, are relatively high may
also preclude any push for a higher retirement age. Between 1960 and 1974,
the unemployment rate in that country was, on the average, below 1 percent.
By 1975 it had jumped to 4.4 percent, and then stabilized until 1979 at over 3
percent, but is presently increasing. (Among persons 60–65, the unemployment rate was almost double that of the total population.) To this must be
added a substantial labor reserve which, as Eichner and Grossjohann point
out, consists of a growing supply of women.

Nonetheless, Eichner and Grossjohann do suggest that opportunities for
continued employment may be expanded as a result of a decline in the
number of jobs requiring the specific capabilities of younger workers. Certainly, as far as the German labor force is concerned, such a shift is apparent.
In 1956, 60 percent of the civilian employed population in the Federal Re-

public were blue-collar workers; by 1979 their share had dropped to 50 percent.

In Germany, as in some other countries, a trend toward shorter, more flexible work hours and toward phased retirement should make it easier for older workers to maintain some attachment to the labor force. This assumes, however, that other groups will not be competing with them for a limited number of jobs.

France

Table 4.3 reveals a sharp reduction in the labor-force participation rates of men and women 60 and older, and particularly 65 and older, in France between 1954 and 1978. For certain age groups (such as males 65–69), the average annual rate of decline in participation began to speed up after the recession of the mid-1970s. Consequently, the savings that pension schemes might have realized as a result of the aging and retirement of the smaller cohorts of 1915–1919 were sharply reduced by "a quick speeding up of early retirements" (Paillat and Chesnais, 1980, p. 21). The French co-researchers express considerable concern over the financial status of pension funds in that country. As in Germany, some systems have been losing contributors while bearing the burden of an increasing number of beneficiaries. For example, the general scheme, which covers wage earners in industry and com-

Table 4.3. Labor-Force Participation Rates for Men and Women 50 Years Old and Older, France, 1954, 1973, and 1978

Sex and	PERCENT			% Change
Age	1954	1973	1978	1954–1978
Men:				
50–54	94.5	93.7	93.2	−1.4
55–59	84.0	82.3	82.1	−2.3
60–64	71.5	61.8	43.6	−39.0
65–69	52.5	22.8	16.0	−69.5
70–74	35.0	8.5	6.5	−81.4
75+	18.5	3.7	2.9	−84.3
Women:				
50–54	46.0	51.2	51.2	+11.3
55–59	43.0	42.9	45.3	+5.3
60–64	35.0	32.5	23.9	−31.7
65–69	22.0	11.8	8.7	−60.4
70–74	13.0	4.7	2.8	−78.5
75+	8.5	2.0	1.4	−83.5

Source: Paillat and Chesnais, 1980.

merce, experienced a regular expansion through 1973. Between 1973 and 1977, however, a loss of 500,000 units of contributors was noted (versus a one million gain during the preceding four years). During this period, the number of beneficiaries grew faster than previously. Trends have been similar in other French pension schemes; for example, for farmers and in special schemes that cover declining occupational groups.

Demands on French pension systems, however, have not necessarily resulted from an increase in persons reaching pensionable age. Instead, "the principal reason explaining financial problems experienced by pension funds is the sudden speeding up of final cessation of employment [for example. early retirement] due to the economic recessions" (Paillat and Chesnais, 1980, p. 11). Long-term declines in the activity rates of persons 60–64 and 65–69, for example, tended to accelerate after 1973.

Slower economic growth is expected to further the decline in activity rates among older workers for some time. In France, the negative economic effects of this may be offset by the labor-force entry, until the end of the 1980s, of large young cohorts. The French project an increase of 3.5 million in the number of potentially active persons between 1975 and 1990, most of which is due to the growth of the younger population, followed by the expansion of female activity.

Paillat and Chesnais contend that employers in France, faced with heavier social charges, tend to reduce their work force by encouraging older workers to retire in order, when possible, to hire younger, better trained, and presumably more productive younger workers. Employers may also reduce the hours worked, by hiring new individuals (young persons and women) on a temporary or part-time basis. If this is indeed what is happening, then the end result would be a "larger number of retired old workers financially supported by a bigger labor supply and by a steady increase of the productivity rate" (Paillat and Chesnais, 1980, p. 30) which, on the surface, appears to be a positive development and one not conducive to raising retirement age.

The French researchers caution, however, that, among other developments, any reduction in the death rate would increase the number of elderly and attendant costs beyond current projections. In addition, as a result of the maturation of the pension systems and efforts to reduce discrimination against women and members of some occupations, pension benefits may increase faster than salaries. Should productivity not increase sufficiently, these trends may, they warn, yield an unbearable tax threshold. At the present time, however, that does not appear to be a problem in France.

The United Kingdom

In the United Kingdom, high unemployment seems to be operating to the disadvantage of older workers who wish to remain in the labor force. The labor force participation rates of men 60–64 in the United Kingdom have been declining since the mid-1970s, although they remain considerably more active than men in some countries, namely, France, Germany, and the United States.

As of 1978, 75.8 percent of the UK males in this age group were in the labor force, down from 82 percent in 1974 (Fogarty, 1980b). To some extent, the Job Release Scheme, whereby workers near retirement age may receive a pre-pension if they are replaced by a recruit from the unemployment register, accounts for some of this withdrawal (about one-fifth of the increase in retirements in 1978, according to Fogarty, 1980b). Fogarty, however, maintains that the main reason for the increase in the proportion of younger "retirees"[5] is the increase in unemployment among older workers and, especially, the "sharply diminished prospect, in the face of high general unemployment, of their getting back into work" (Fogarty, 1980b, p. 17). In contrast to what appears to be the case in some other countries, these retirement trends cannot be explained by increased availability of occupational pensions, according to a study by the Department of Ministry.[6] Nor is there any reason to assume that ill health—always a significant cause of early retirement—has increased in importance in recent years.

Fogarty (1980a) points out that during periods of high employment, it is relatively easy for the young old to remain active. Yet, in the United Kingdom, there has been a "striking contrast" in the way that women and persons of pension age (traditionally members of the "secondary" work force) took advantage of the favorable employment opportunities from World War II through the 1960s. Married women pressed ahead and established themselves as an accepted part of the work force, while older persons did not. (Britain has one of the highest rates of employed married women in Europe.) Women also achieved the backing of legislation against sex discrimination in the 1970s. Older workers, on the other hand, did not "establish themselves this way" (Fogarty, 1980a, p. 48). Consequently, the employment prospects for persons of pensionable age are anything but good in the United Kingdom, where the unemployment rate had been running about 5 to 6 percent since 1977. In addition, the situation over the near future looks no better: restricted growth is likely to characterize the economy, and unemployment rates are expected to rise through the early 1980s; indeed, the unemployment rate had reached 10 percent by early 1981.[7]

The United Kingdom projects continued decline in activity rates through 1991 among men 65 and older and among nonmarried women 60-plus. In contrast to these two groups, rates for older married women are projected to increase. Because the population above pension age is expected to increase only slightly between 1977 and 1991 (by some 300,000 people) and then to decline, while the active population is expected to increase by about 2.2 million persons, the labor-force-dependency burden (like the crude population dependency burden) will improve considerably over the next decade. Nonetheless, as pointed out previously, an increase in the number of very old will add to the overall financial dependency burden.

Denmark

The trend of steadily declining labor-force participation rates on the part of older males has not been observed in all countries. Denmark represents a significant and interesting deviation. At first glance, it would appear that labor-force trends in Denmark are comparable to those in the United States and other European nations: the final column in table 4.4 reveals a decline in labor-force activity rates for men aged 50 to 74 between 1960 and 1978; the higher the age, the greater the deterioration, although the long-term trend had certainly been in the direction of reduced participation for all.

This overall decline, however, does not reflect a steady decrease. In contrast to France, for one, where older-worker labor-force withdrawal accelerated at a more rapid rate during and after the recession of 1973/1974, labor-force participation rates in Denmark not only were maintained, but actually increased somewhat through 1978. This occurred in spite of the fact that "drastically increasing unemployment" had set in (Friis and Hansen, 1980).[8]

The employment situation of the elderly in Denmark, however, has not been quite as propitious as the rates in table 4.4 would suggest. Unemployment rates among the elderly also increased, and Friis and Hansen speculate that there were relatively more long-term unemployed among the older labor-force participants. The introduction of the severance pay scheme in January 1979 has precipitated a drastic decline in labor-force participation among 60- to 64-year-old men. From a level of 79 percent in 1978, the participation rate for this age group fell to 62 percent in 1979. Among men 65–69, labor-force participation rates dropped from 45 to 34 percent in that one-year period. Furthermore, participation rates among these two age groups are expected to continue to fall through 1995, after which they are projected to remain more or less unchanged. (Severance pay should have less of an impact on persons 65-plus than on younger persons, since only the first two years—65 and 66—are covered by the scheme.)

Nonetheless, forecasts to the year 2000 paint a very optimistic picture of the labor force through the turn of the century in Denmark. Participation rates are projected to decline somewhat among men aged 20–59, and to increase—sharply in some instances—among all groups of women between the ages of 29 and 74. Only among men 60–74 does the Danish Ministry of Finance project a decline in activity. The significant fact is that, overall, labor-force participation rates are projected to *increase* between 1979 and 2000: in the case of men 15 and older, they remain constant at 79 percent; among women, they are projected to increase from 61 to 72 percent.

Table 4.4. Labor-Force Participation Rates for Men and Women 50–74 Years Old, Denmark, 1960–1978

Sex and Age	1960	1965	1970	1972	PERCENT 1973	1974	1975	1976	1977	1978	% Change 1960–1978
Men:											
50–54	97	98	95	93	93	93	93	94	94	94	−3.1
55–59	95	96	91	88	87	88	89	89	90	89	−6.3
60–64	88	89	81	78	76	76	79	78	79	79	−10.2
65–69	58	60	47	45	45	46	46	47	47	45	−22.4
70–74	28	26	14	14	15	17	16	16	17	15	−46.4
Women:											
50–54	37	45	51	59	61	60	62	62	63	64	+73.0
55–59	34	40	41	48	49	50	49	49	53	54	+58.8
60–64	23	28	26	30	30	33	32	33	34	35	+52.2
65–69	12	14	11	12	11	12	13	12	12	14	+16.7
70–74	6	6	4	4	5	5	4	3	4	4	−33.3

SOURCE: Friis and Hansen, 1980.

Overall, the labor force will be larger in the year 2000 by about 340,000 persons, reflecting an average annual increase of about 1 percent between 1979 and 1990 and about 0.5 percent between 1990 and 2000. Consequently, the total dependency ratio, based on the ratio of inactive persons to the active (labor-force) population, will decline steadily and sharply (from 95 to 79 percent) if the Danish projections hold out.

The cloud on the horizon is the projected decline in activity rates of older men (60 and above) at least through 1990 or 1995, and the increase in the number of elderly, especially those 75-plus, who will have to be provided for. These developments, as the Danish report highlights, emphasize the importance of women workers in counteracting the problems of an aging population.

WOMEN AS AN OFFSET

From the Danish report, one gets the impression that the projected increase in female employment will more than offset any support burden evolving from a growing older, nonworking population. In terms of numbers alone, an offset does exist. However, a labor-force body count alone is only slightly more informative here than in discussions of crude dependency ratios based on population data alone. What counts is whether the tax contribution of these female workers is comparable to the lost contributions from male retirees and the cost of their retirement. The size of those contributions depends primarily on salary and hours worked; the increase in part-time female employment has been particularly noticeable.

Two of the other European reports, as well as data from the United States, strongly suggest that the projected increases in female labor-force participation—in the short-run, in any case—will not fully compensate for the decline among middle-aged and older men. Nor will it serve to stabilize the dependency ratio. In the United States, for example, where women have made considerable progress in the labor market, equality in employment status, earnings, and work schedules remains an elusive goal. The majority of part-time workers are women, and their share of the part-time labor force has been increasing. To be sure, many of these women are voluntary part-time workers, but the fact that they work part-time by choice is irrelevant when it comes to an assessment of their social security contributions vis-à-vis those of men.

Similar, although more striking, trends are evident in Sweden, where almost all of the increase in female activity rates has consisted of part-time employment. Between 1965 and 1978, the proportion of full-time female workers remained almost unchanged. In addition, the increase in female employment has also been accompanied by an increase in absence from work (Berglind and Bergroth, 1980).

Like Berglind and Bergroth in Sweden, the German co-researchers stress a need for special measures (such as more part-time work) if the female participation rate is to be augmented (Eichner and Grossjohann, 1980). Currently, women in Germany have a labor-force participation rate of 38 percent and are, hence, considered of "significant importance." Nonetheless, women are, as a rule, relegated to lower-paying and less skilled jobs, denied access to technical positions, and are offered fewer opportunities for retraining—despite legal entitlement to equality. Moreover, their work life is typically discontinuous, and reentry is apparently difficult for the German female, as it is for women in the United States.

If, however, structural difficulties are overcome and women can be assisted in adapting to job requirements, it is believed that female labor-force participation could reach 80 percent by 2010 and "fully compensate" for any decline in participation on the part of older age groups. This appears to be a rather optimistic statement, for which no supporting evidence was provided.

SUMMARY

The overall consensus from the country reports is that the dependency burden, this time as measured by labor-force participation rates, is probably manageable over the next decade or perhaps longer. Estimates and projections from the International Labour Office tend to support this conclusion. Table 4.5 presents dependency ratios for each of the five European countries, based on estimated and projected labor-force participation rates for persons 64 and younger. An assumption is made that all persons 65 and older have

Table 4.5. Ratio of Persons 65-plus to Labor-Force Participants Under Age 65, 1950–2000[1] (Actual and Projected)

	Denmark	France	Germany (FR)	Sweden	United Kingdom	United States
1950	20	26	21	24	24	20
1955	22	27	22	26	25	22
1960	24	29	24	29	26	24
1965	25	30	27	30	26	24
1970	27	32	31	32	29	24
1975	29	32	32	35	30	24
1980	31	32	32	37	32	24
1985	31	28	28	37	31	25
1990	31	30	29	37	31	25
2000	30	31	32	32	28	24

SOURCE: International Labour Office, 1977, from data in tables 2 and 5. Projections from 1975 on.

[1] Number of elderly per 100 labor force participants younger than 65.

been, and will remain, inactive. Since some older persons—albeit a minority—do remain in the labor force, these ratios slightly overestimate the magnitude of the dependency ratio.[9] The result may be compensated by an
increasing number of older workers who leave the labor force before age 65.

In each country, this dependency ratio increased appreciably between
1950 and 1975, in large part because of the increase in the older population.
Projections for subsequent years, however, reveal no, or relatively moderate,
increases between 1975 and 2000 in all of those countries, and an eventual
drop (also minor to fairly steep) of varying duration in all of them.

Whether pressures for more and better retirement benefits on the part of
the population 65-plus in these countries will aggravate what appears to be
rather favorable projections (supported, for the most part, by the country
reports) remains to be seen. Such projections, however, would not augur well
for the success of any efforts to prolong working life, especially in the face of
increasing demands of young and female labor-force entrants and reentrants.

5

An Aging Population and the Social Security System

Despite the rather favorable outlook with regard to labor-force participation and dependency ratios over the next 20 years, all five countries face growing demands on their retirement income systems, social security in particular. As noted previously, liberalization of benefits, expanded coverage, and increasing longevity have increased the size and number of pension benefits.

In all five countries, working life has been shortened by later entry into the labor force (resulting from a longer period of education) and the secular trend toward early retirement, both of which have reduced the number of contributions and aggravated demands on social security systems.

Definitions of social security and social expenditures differ within a country as well as among countries. National data and compilations by the International Labour Office, the Organization of Economic Cooperation and Development, the European Economic Commission, and the Council of Europe also use differing definitions of social security. Add to this the fact that specific data for expenditures for the aged by age and sex are missing or incomplete in many cases, and it becomes evident that an international comparison in the strictest sense is impossible. However, each compilation of data, from whatever source, reveals trends over time that allow one to gain some feel for the demographic and socioeconomic developments. These trends are substantially similar in all countries under study.

CHARACTERISTICS OF THE GOVERNMENT PENSION PROGRAMS

Each of the five European countries covered by this study has a well-established social security system that yields retirement benefits. Some of the working papers prepared by the European co-researchers distinguish between statutory (normal) pensionable age, the minimum age at which the insured can retire with full or reduced old age benefits, and the average actual retirement age. All the countries also provide for delayed retirement, which yields higher pensions for the insured.

The structures of the government pension programs differ somewhat among the five countries. The French and the West German systems come nearest to that of the United States. The German program, which provides relatively high benefits, is basically a contributory, earnings-related system: the government subsidized only about 16 percent of the cost in 1979 and 1980; for 1981, the administration proposed shifting a large part or all of the pension subsidy to the unemployment insurance program. The German program is supplemented by private pensions covering about two-thirds of the employed.

The French general system is fully financed by contributions from employees and employers, and also provides an appreciable earnings-related pension to the insured. On top of it, employees are also covered by compulsory private pension systems. Together, these systems yield a relatively high retirement income.

The United Kingdom pension has a basic flat-rate component topped by an earnings-related component, which can, however, be "contracted out"; this means that an equivalent or better-paying private ("occupational") pension can be substituted for the earnings-related portion. In Denmark, the work-related contributory pension represents a second layer on top of a "universal" pension covering all qualifying residents. Since the work-related pension is small and not inflation-proofed, private pension schemes offer additional protection for those 25 percent of the salaried workers who have established them through collective bargaining or agreements with individual employers. Very few nonsalaried workers have private pensions.

Sweden's structure is probably the most complicated. Sweden also has a universal pension covering all aged citizens, which is supplemented by an earnings-related, entirely employer-financed benefit, whose introduction in 1960 was quite stormy; it almost failed to pass the parliament, and finally passed with a one-vote majority. The majority of Swedish blue- and white-collar workers also benefit from nationwide pensions based upon national collective-bargaining agreements. In a few cases, a fourth layer—private pensions financed by the enterprise for high-management personnel—is available.

Ninety percent of the basic (universal) pension benefit amounts in Denmark, and 43 percent in Sweden, are financed from general revenues. Workers in Denmark and employers in Sweden contribute the remainder through a payroll tax on the insured worker's earnings up to a certain limit. In two other countries, West Germany and the United Kingdom, the government contributes relatively small amounts to the pensions, which the retired worker receives as a matter of right. In all five countries, national, and occasionally local, governments as a rule carry the entire cost of supplementary, means-tested allowances (public assistance or welfare payments) to those aged who have no claims to social security old-age insurance benefits or whose benefits are insufficient.

From one viewpoint, the distinction between the various sources of income for the pension programs is not all that important. Since all five basic public programs, as well as the French and Swedish complementary private pension systems, are currently financed on a pay-as-you-go basis (that is, they do not use capital funding), the currently active population is forced to transfer some of its earnings to the retired (intergenerational transfer). Whether this sacrifice is made through higher income taxes and special taxes or through a social security payroll tax is, in the end, of no great significance. In both cases, the contributor's ability to consume, save, and invest is curtailed.

Social security contributions are, however, often perceived differently from other taxes. The term "social security insurance" has created—and the systems have benefited from—the myth that the government pension is not a transfer payment, but an enforceable individual right to a contractual pension. Those who (wrongly) envisage social security contributions as insurance premiums accumulated in their personal earmarked insurance accounts may offer no or less tax resistance to the social security payroll levy than to other types of taxes. Others, like some of the Swedish, Danish, and German workers, see in social security their own and their union's hard-won victory gaining them income security in their old age that is "comparable in nature, if not in amount, to what the rich can provide." These workers also appear willing to shoulder higher contributions. Such attitudes on the part of the workers are even stronger when, as in Sweden, the payroll tax is levied, not on the worker, but on the employer. In this case, the cost to the worker (such as higher prices or lower wages) may not always be fully understood.

Where the social myth of insurance premium has been dispelled, or where contributions of workers have repeatedly been raised substantially over short intervals, the increasing burden may create dissatisfaction. This holds particularly true if real earnings decline. In the case of falling profits, management also objects to rising social security contributions as another inroad on its liquidity and ultimately its economic status. That portion of the social security payroll tax that finances retirement benefits is especially vulnerable in the case of young workers far from retirement, the higher-paid employees who, under some benefit formulae, can only expect a proportionally smaller state pension than their less well paid co-workers, and those who lose confidence in the state program's future ability and willingness to provide them with their "earned" pension. This potential *crise de confiance* has encouraged social security planners to look to other sources of financing the growing pension load—in particular, to the state's general revenues.

The increase in general taxes, attributable to the need for mounting state contributions to partially or fully state-financed government pension programs, meets less specific opposition, but faces the general tax revolt, as exemplified by such intermittently popular leaders as Mogen Gilstrup in Denmark, Anders Lange in Norway, or Kemp and Roth in the United

Table 5.1. Change in Combined Tax and Social Security Contributions as Percentage of GNP at Market Prices

	1963	1970	1972	1974	1976	1978
Denmark	24.9	35.4	40.6	41.7	40.0	41.9
France	34.0	38.4	37.1	35.6	39.1	40.8
Germany (FR)	34.0	33.3	35.1	36.6	37.9	39.0
Sweden	34.9	39.9	44.8	44.7	50.1	53.2
United Kingdom	29.8	37.9	34.7	35.6	36.2	34.2
United States	27.8	28.7	30.4	31.3	29.1	30.2

SOURCE: Miegel, 1981, Table 1. Reprinted by permission of Verlag BONN AKTUELL.

States. Table 5.1 provides a glimpse of the trend (generally upward) in combined tax and social security contributions as a percentage of GNP at market prices. The percentage (again, generally upward) of gross domestic production channeled through government in four of the five European countries and in the United States can be seen in table 5.2. Proponents of the tax revolt quite often hold the "excesses" of the welfare state responsible for some of the lack of economic growth. Criticism centers upon transfer and welfare programs, particularly public assistance to the poor, of which the aged constitute a significant part in all countries. This may spill over into the old-age pension program which is attacked for the size of the benefit, the cost, the wastefulness, and the size of its bureaucracy.[1]

THE GROWTH OF SOCIAL SECURITY EXPENDITURES

Attacks on the government social security pension programs hit the systems at a time when they find themselves in financial difficulties. This is clearly evident in Germany and the United States, recognized in the United Kingdom, and real but concealed in France (where expenditures for the aged amounted to 20 percent of all public cost in 1978). In the United Kingdom and Sweden, attempts to reduce public pension expenditures have so far been moderated by a fairly calm identification of the various factors leading to the increasing demands on the social security pension program, and by taking full account of the basic popularity of this income-maintenance device.

In addition to the deteriorating contributor/beneficiary ratio, we shall refer subsequently to expanded coverage, the rise in benefit level, and the adjustment of benefits to price and/or wage changes (inflation-proofing) in the prosperous 1950s and 1960s as another group of factors leading to increased social security expenditures and consumption. In Sweden, with maturation of the earnings-related pension, total pensioners' consumption rose

Table 5.2. Total Public Expenditures as Percent of GDP at Market Prices

	1965	1970	1975	1977
Denmark	31	40	46	46
Germany (FR)	37	38	48	47
Sweden	35	43	52	62
United Kingdom[1]	37	41	50	44
United States[1]	27	32	35	33

SOURCE: Geiger, *Welfare and Efficiency*, Washington, 1978, Table 1.1. Reprinted by permission of National Planning Association.
[1] British and U.S. figures for 1977 show the effect of a policy to reduce public expenditures after 1975.

by 7.5 percent annually between 1975 and 1980. Their share as a percentage of total private consumption increased over the same period from 13 to 17 percent, and was expected to reach the 20 percent level by 1985.

In Denmark, where pensions are financed by taxes on employers and workers, any shortfall between the earmarked tax revenues and expenditures must be met by the general revenues of the nation. Although there is no evidence of a general opposition to the increasing cost of this protection or to the need to supplement revenues to meet the growing cost of old-age pensions and services for the elderly, opposition to the rising total tax level has found political expression. This rising tax level, we might emphasize, has been caused to some extent by a higher rate of subsidization of expenditures for the aged.

In all five European countries, as in the United States, the level of pension expenditures increased more than that of prices or wages over those years. For example, French pensions increased 1.5 times faster than wages between 1966 and 1978. Taking the respective levels of prices, wages, and old-age expenditures in 1966 in France as 100, one finds that prices, wages, and old-age expenditures had risen to 225, 400, and 576, respectively. While prices rose in 1974 by 13.7 percent, wages rose by 17.3 percent. (By 1979 the trend had reversed: prices rose by 10.8 percent, but wages by only 9.2 percent.) On the other hand, these expenditures also replaced an increasing percentage of the pre-retirement income.

In Sweden, the portion of total household income consisting of pensions rose from 6 percent in 1975 to 12 percent in 1977. Elsewhere, retirement pensions also represent an increasing percentage of the household income of the retired and have substantially reduced the number of aged poor, as evidenced by the decline of the percentage of retired who are in need of means- or income-tested supplementary assistance. In Sweden, for example, 13 percent of all social-assistance beneficiaries were aged (67-plus) in 1965; by 1974, the aged comprised only 5 percent of the assistance population.

Table 5.3. Indices of Annual Average Benefit Expenditure Per Head of the Total Population[1]

	1960	1965	1970	1972	1973	1974
Denmark	43	61	100	130	140	144
France	56	84	100	140	150	156
Germany (FR)	60	77	100	119	125	137
Sweden	39	62	100	112	119	140
United Kingdom	63	77	100	107	114	115
United States	53	65	100	124	134	137

SOURCE: International Labour Office, 1979a, table 4, pp. 68–69. (Copyright 1979, ILO, Geneva). The nearly static relation (discussed in text) of pension to total social security benefit expenditures for the relevant years was computed on the basis of tables 5 and 8.
[1] Values adjusted to the cost-of-living indices: 1970 = 100.

Since the ratios of pension expenditures to total social security expenditures differ little over the years—in Europe old-age pensions consumed two-fifths, and together with disability pensions, one-half, of total social security payments (ILO, 1979a)—the trend in the development of pensions can be deduced from the latter. Tables 5.3 and 5.4 eliminate the effects of inflation by relating the sum of all social security benefits to the consumer price index (1970 = 100) and relating total social security expenditures to the gross domestic product at purchasers' prices for each year.

Table 5.3 reveals a constant rise on a per capita basis in all benefits, including retirement, in the five European countries and the United States, during a period which reflects the prosperity of the late 1950s and 1960s. Higher benefits are expressed in higher expenditures in real terms. If they exceed the growth of other components in the national accounts, particularly that of earnings, their ratio to the domestic national product rises. This can be seen in table 5.4.

The Statistical Office of the European Economic Commission attempted to show the changes in expenditures for old-age pensions alone between 1975

Table 5.4. Social Security Expenditures as Percentage of Gross Domestic Product

Country	1960	1965	1970	1974
Denmark	11.7	12.2	16.6	21.0
France	13.2	15.6	15.3	21.6
Germany (FR)	15.5	16.5	16.8	20.3
Sweden	10.9	13.6	18.8	24.4
United Kingdom	10.8	11.7	13.8	14.6
United States	7.0	7.6	9.9	12.5

SOURCE: International Labour Office, 1979a, Table 2, pp. 56–59. (Copyright 1979, ILO, Geneva).

As can be seen, the growth of total social security expenditures, including pension expenditures, is quite remarkable for the period 1960–1974. The percentage continued to rise. By 1979, it reached 25 percent in France and 30 percent in Sweden.

Table 5.5. Expenditures for Old-Age Pensions as Percent of Gross Domestic Product

	Country			
Year	Germany (FR)	Sweden	France	United Kingdom
1960	7.2	2.8	5.0	3.4
1971	8.0	3.4	6.8	4.7
1975	11.2	na	9.1	9.2
1980	11.2	na	10.5	8.2

SOURCE: Figures for 1960 and 1971 from Rohrlich, 1980, p. 84; figures for 1975 and 1980 from the Commission of the European Communities, 1980.

and 1980 for a small number of member countries of the Common Market (table 5.5). These have been supplemented by data for earlier years from Rohrlich (1980). In the European countries shown in this table, old-age expenditures as a percent of gross domestic product (GDP) have tended to rise steadily since 1960. Expenditures increased by 56 percent in Germany and more than doubled in France and the United Kingdom (although the 1980 figure for the latter is somewhat lower than the one for 1975). This rise owes as much to the growing number of beneficiaries in maturing programs as to the liberalization of the benefit structure, particularly noticeable in France and the United Kingdom.

The Danish country report relates public expenditures for the aged (including pensions and services) to gross national product (Friis and Hansen, 1980); in that country expenditures rose from 5.5 percent to 12.7 percent between 1964 and 1979. In France, OASD pensions increased from 36.5 percent to 42.8 percent of "social incomes" between 1966 and 1978. In terms of the gross domestic product, these expenditures rose from 5 percent in 1962 to 6.8 percent in 1971. Between 1960 and 1971, the total pension-expenditure-increase amounted to 13.1 percent. Over this 11-year period, the GDP increased by only 5 percent in real terms. By 1975, the cost of the Swedish pension (including disabilities) had reached 10 percent of gross national product (GNP), up from 5 percent in 1960.

In the predominantly contributory systems, the growth of the benefit burden brought about an increase in the payroll tax rate and the tax base. Between 1973 and 1978, the contribution rate increased by 27 percent (employer, 34 percent; worker, 15 percent) in France. In Sweden, where the financing falls entirely upon the employers, their contribution rate jumped by 93 percent.

Until recently, the affected workers accepted the increased burden with equanimity. This was largely due to the simultaneous growth of earnings and to the fact that the benefits came nearer to providing an adequate retirement income. The adequacy of retirement pay is typically expressed by its replacement value, the degree to which the pension replaces pre-retirement

Table 5.6. Earnings-Replacement Rates of Old-Age Benefits 1965–75

Country	Single Worker						Aged Couple					
	1965	1969	1972	1973	1974	1975	1965	1969	1972	1973	1974	1975
Denmark	35	29	30	30	30	29	51	42	44	44	43	43
France	49	42	44	47	44	46	65	56	60	62	60	65
Germany (FR)	48	56	49	49	49	50	48	56	49	49	49	50
Sweden	31	39	45	45	50	59	44	52	58	57	62	76
United Kingdom	23	21	22	22	22	26	36	33	34	33	33	39
United States	29	29	34	38	36	38	44	44	50	57	54	57

SOURCE: Haanes-Olsen, 1978, pp. 3–14. For the definitions and methodology used in this table, see Horlick, 1970, pp. 3–16. Rates for men with average earnings in manufacturing.

A less accurate measure of replacement rates relates them to average industrial earnings. However, this method, used by W.A.R. Escombe (summary in *Pensions World* and cited in Fogarty, 1980a) shows nearly identical trends for a married couple. For 1977, Sweden leads pension replacement at 75 percent, followed by France at 58 percent and Germany at 50 percent.

income. The change (growth) in the replacement rates is presented in table 5.6. The more recent replacement rates provided by the background papers of the European co-researchers are appreciably higher, since some of the systems had not reached the same grade of maturity between 1965 and 1975, as they are expected to do later on. For instance, United Kingdom claims of an average 50 to 55 percent replacement rate will only be obtainable by the end of the century, when the earnings-related state pension will have matured.

Table 5.6 does not include the contribution of private pensions. In 1979, the French claimed to have reached a replacement rate of 50 percent for the public pension and of 20 percent for the private pension, for a total of 70 percent of wages under the social security ceiling. The Germans speak of a replacement value of almost 74 percent of net (52 percent of gross) earnings for workers with 45 years of contributions.

Some of these rates in table 5.6 refer to long-service employees with 30, 37.5, and 40 years of service. For the sake of comparison, figures in table 5.6 are calculated in terms of a hypothetical average worker. The entries suffice, however, to display the great advance in the adequacy of old-age benefits for aged couples which characterized that period. The decline of the replacement rate for single Danish workers between 1965 and 1975 resulted from a deliberate policy to shift the emphasis toward maintaining the value of the pension for the aged couple. The most significant gains were made in Sweden, followed by the United States.

INFLATION-PROOFING

The value of the social security pension was further enhanced by its inflation-proofing. By the late 1970s, semi- or fully automatic adjustment of benefits on the basis of price and/or wage indices in all five European systems and the United States protected pensioners against the effects of inflation on purchasing power and/or economic status. In cases where wage-level changes limped behind sharp inflationary increases in the cost of living, adjustment to price-level changes put pensioners in a more favorable position than that available to active workers, a fact that helped to render the adjustment process vulnerable. (Private pensions were, in nearly all cases, not able to match fully—if at all—the protection of state pensions against the devaluation of the currency, an important aspect of income maintenance of the retired.) The resulting augmentation of the benefit expenditures under high inflation rates, which in some cases reached double digits (United Kingdom, United States, Denmark), is well established in the reports prepared by our European co-researchers.

The substantial rise in benefit expenditures was further increased because the various earnings-related systems reached or neared maturity. Maturity is the time when all or most retirees meet all the qualifications in terms of length of affiliation with, or number of contributions to, the pension scheme, thus assuring them a full (as distinguished from a transitional, sometimes proportionally smaller) pension. This held true, for instance, for two-thirds of the Swedish (second-tier) state earnings-related program of 1960–1962. The French general system neared the halfway mark; the German system had already reached maturity; and the United States system treated all involved almost as if they had been fully insured. Only the United Kingdom earnings-related pension, which entered in force in April 1978, was still at the beginning of development.

EARLY RETIREMENT

One of the factors that significantly increased the benefit load was not fully foreseen, namely, the enormous popularity of the various early retirement provisions enacted in the late 1960s and 1970s, which swelled the number of beneficiaries and led to a rise in the length of pension payments for up to five years. Actuarially reduced pensions had been available for some time in France (five years before full retirement age after 10 years of contributions), Sweden (five years before full retirement age), and the United States (at age 62, three years before full retirement age). Those were much used, but by their very nature, did not affect the magnitude of pension expenditures. More workers than expected began to avail themselves of a variety of early labor-force-withdrawal options. These included: a full pension at age 63 for a German long-service employee (35 years) and qualifying women at age 60; various programs including a partial pension for a part-time Swedish worker between the ages of 60 and 64; an unemployment (pre-retirement) benefit substantially higher than a pension for French workers who quit the labor market; a similar, but not decreasing, benefit under the United Kingdom Job Release Program[2]; and a severance pay scheme in Denmark.[3] No study has reported the relative weight of the various factors which determine the insured's early retirement decision.[4]

Paillat and Chesnais (1980) have attempted to assign relative weights to the major factors that produced the rise in French payroll taxes levied upon contributors in the general scheme to finance retirement pensions between 1960 and 1977. They conclude that in their country: the aging of the population has affected that rise by 11 percent; early retirement accounts for 33 percent; and the adjustments of the pension contributed 56 percent; for a total of 100 percent. This led the Commissariat du Plan in *Vieillir demain* (Commissariat Général du Plan, 1980) to the conclusion that the aging of the population has not been and will not be the principal cause of the increase in pension outlays in the near future, although this limited role of population aging cannot be taken for granted over the long run.

The United Kingdom paper also denies the importance of demographic changes for this century. It sees the cause in already agreed-upon and expected liberalization of benefits of all sorts. With the exogenous fertility factor out of the way (which responds only very inadequately to government policies) and inflation-caused pension adjustment hardly a politically acceptable target for the reduction in income-security-conscious France, this, as of now, leaves only early retirement as a target for future reduction of expenditures in that country. No other country has made such an assessment of the causes of the rise in social security expenditures. Historical data, are, of course, a poor guide for the period following the year 2000, when the age distribution and the ratio of contributors to pensioners are likely to cause more severe increases in real per capita social security expenditures in France and elsewhere. However, the French attempt highlights the need for such analyses (Paillat and Chesnais, 1980).

REDUCED SOCIAL SECURITY INCOME

The revenues of the social security pension program were affected most by the increasing rates of unemployment in all countries under study. Unemployment was particularly high in the United Kingdom and Denmark. In West Germany, the Federal Labor Office, which administers unemployment insurance, continued to pay old-age insurance contributions for its clients. Unemployment, therefore, had no effect upon the revenues of that system. It did, however, add to its expenditures, because persons between ages 60 and 64 could instead claim a retirement pension if they remained unemployed for 12 months in an 18-month period. Lowered fertility was to reduce the active labor market (the contributors) only much later. The French working paper allocates a 75 percent share of the deterioration of the ratio of pensioners to contributors between 1973 and 1977 to unemployment, and 25 percent to early retirement (Paillat and Chesnais, 1980). As more and more workers availed themselves of the early retirement option, social security revenues shrank.

6

The Social Security Financing Question: The Range of Remedial Actions

The sharp increase in pension expenditures, which coincided with an equally sharp decrease in revenues, made itself felt in the decline of the contingency reserve funds of social security systems in Europe. Never very high in systems based on current financing (they ranged from three-months' to one-years' expenditures), their complete depletion in a short time could easily be foreseen.

Two types of questions arose: (1) Which of the various factors leading to the rise in expenditures were exogenous and, hence, not subject to remedial action by the social security program; which could be curbed? (2) What methods should be used in the short and long run to replenish reserve funds and bring revenues and expenditures in a long-term balance?

Inflation and unemployment are exogenous factors. Although it could be hoped that their increase was of a short-run nature, this hope weakened as both continued on their upward course. The inability to deal effectively and lastingly with inflation, the conflicting advice offered by monetarists and neo-Keynesians, and the poor results of the few measures taken, are clearly expressed in the quite modest governmental forecasts of productivity and economic growth rates for the next 20 and more years. In all countries under study, these rates are expected to fall well below those prevailing in the preceding decades. This point is clearly brought out in the Swedish paper (Berglind and Bergroth, 1980). Since the economic growth of that country depends upon increased exports, necessitating large investments, only a very small proportion of the increased GNP is available for improved consumption. So much of the small increase in private expenditures is already earmarked for statutory pension payments, maturing in 1990, that near-zero growth can be allotted to the remainder.

The suspicion arises that the generally accepted view of the unreliability of long-term economic growth and fertility projections may also serve as a shield against future critique. Because of these uncertainties, social security pension planning, which must take into account the long-run development of earnings, employment, demographic changes, and so forth, is badly served. Improvement in inflation and unemployment rates requires actions that lie beyond the capability of a pension program. Such actions are difficult to achieve in the European economies, whose performance depends to such a high degree upon the ability to export in an uncontrollable world market. Some of the European co-researchers see hope in high-technology exports as the one field where these countries are likely to maintain and increase their comparative advantage, while former export leaders, like textiles, will decline, unable to compete with the products of the developing and emerging countries. Several of the European country reports and the International Labour Office see the employment opportunities of older and retired workers precisely in the declining industries with relatively low productivity and wages.

REMEDIAL ACTION TO SOLVE LONG-TERM PROBLEMS

More radical remedies, such as replacing the social security pension with a means-tested system—perhaps in the form of a negative-income-tax program—are deemed politically unobtainable (a United Kingdom tax-credit scheme has been discussed, but not yet been enacted) and are, presumably for that reason, not even mentioned in the five European reports. One participant at the Swedish seminar on retirement-age policy raised the question: What is more important: retained and improved buying power, or more and better care and services? He failed to provide an answer, thereby acknowledging that retrenchment may affect services first, and that services are no substitute for statutory or contractual pensions. The five countries accept the existing major income-maintenance mechanisms and their main purposes. They distinguish the problem of meeting the future demands that an increasingly aging European population will pose for these programs and the economy, from that of restoring their financial balance now. These questions also arise for some of the special pension schemes, such as those for agricultural workers, farmers, and seamen, which in addition suffer from industry-specific problems.

INCREASED REVENUES

Immediate measures that are proposed aim to (1) increase revenues through increasing coverage under the system, raising contribution rates and bases, and seeking additional government financing; and (2) reduce expenditures by lowering benefits. Some of these measures provide only temporary financial relief; others are fairly easily reversible once a financial balance has been established for a reasonable time.

Several other remedies can only be installed over time. Among them are changes in the financing mechanisms (capital funding), reversing the trend toward early retirement, encouraging a longer work life, or compelling such a result by raising the normal pensionable retirement age. In this group, greater reliance also falls upon private pensions and savings. Some of these will be discussed here; others in the following chapters.

MORE CONTRIBUTORS: WOMEN

Expanding coverage entails increasing the number of contributors. One aspect of this approach is based upon the hope that the present trend of increasing the percentage of women who will become active members of the labor force will continue and that they will add to the revenues of social security systems. This applies with special emphasis to women who are freed from the burden of bringing up their children, a group that has shown substantially greater attachment to the labor force in recent years. Although the earnings of women in all five countries are smaller than those of men, which means that contributions based on income from work will be less, the sum of their contributions is likely to offer some early relief to social security finances. What is frequently overlooked, however, is the fact that the same women will also acquire claims against the system that will add to the future pension load. Moreover, female life expectancy in Europe is six to eight years longer than that of men, so pension benefits must be paid for a longer period of time.

Employment of women is, of course, not entirely cost-free to society. For the younger women, there are the costs of creches, day-care centers, and other welfare costs for children that must be considered. Nor will the older women who represent the core of the not-as-yet fully engaged female labor force, or some of the younger ones, be able to care for the aged members of the family to whom they offered unremunerated, informal care. These tasks will be shifted to the society and, hence, add to the total expenses for the aged.

EXTENSIONS TO SPECIAL SCHEMES

Extension of coverage to other labor-force groups so far outside the social security system (such as government employees, workers in quasi-governmental enterprises, and groups covered under special systems) will also offer only temporary financial relief, since they too will ultimately increase the future pension volume. Unless such incorporation leads to reduced benefits for those transferred, shifting to the major pension schemes will not necessarily lower the total national pension burden if the possible administrative cost savings of a unified pension scheme are disregarded. The consolidation of pension systems may decrease administrative costs, unless the major system's administrative capacity has already reached its optimum size and is in danger of being overloaded. In some European countries, consolidation may actually worsen the financial status of the major system. This was the case in Germany (among artisans), and would be the result in France if special systems in declining industries, now in financial distress, were shifted to the general system. A similar problem may arise in the transformation of voluntary to compulsory coverage, unless contribution rates are adequately adjusted. An example is the incorporation of the self-employed into the "general scheme" in France.

FOREIGN WORKERS

For many years the revenues of the general systems were increased by large-scale employment of contributing foreign workers in a tight labor market, who could be counted upon to return to their countries of origin before they qualified for a pension. This device has also lost some of its luster. Persistent unemployment has reduced or stopped the influx of "guest" workers in both Germany and France. In the latter case, the government has so far unsuccessfully subsidized the repatriation of the foreign workers. Xenophobic attitudes on the part of the host country's workers, their unions, and the population in general, as well as difficulties in integrating foreign workers into a different culture, have become stronger. Costly welfare and other policy measures are sometimes required. A large percentage of foreign workers did not leave the new country—even after losing their jobs, but instead settled there with their families in foreign enclaves. By staying on, their own chances (and particularly their descendants' chances) of earning enough credits for pensions in the future cancel out the temporary contribution advantages for the systems' finances (see Otero, 1981, p. 3). Nor are the pension systems helped where international agreements (EEC and Nordic countries) encourage migration but provide for an intergovernmental settlement of contributions and payments to each other's citizens and residents.

HIGHER CONTRIBUTIONS

The traditional method of raising revenues in European social insurance programs is to increase the contribution rate and base in contributory social security systems. This is the case when contributions are the sole or main source of revenue (France, the United States, West Germany, and the United Kingdom) or when they apply only to a second, earnings-related layer (Denmark, Sweden). It is also the case when the burden is placed directly on insured workers and their employers or only on the latter (Sweden). This is one of the solutions used in West Germany, which raised the contribution rate as of January 1, 1981, from 18 percent to 18.5 percent shared equally between workers and employers. This was also used in 1977 in the United States. As suggested above, where there is a strong ideological tie of the social security pension to the labor movement or party, or a sizable retirement benefit commanding widespread popular approval and expectations, such a move will, as a rule, be accepted.[1] We have already mentioned that resistance may well arise, as several country reports point out, if the sum of general taxes and social-insurance contributions substantially decreases the insured's take-home pay (in real terms).[2] This could occur in situations where wages lag behind (inflationary) prices, or when they are subjected to ceilings or wage freezes in pursuit of an income policy to stem inflation while profits soar. Some country observers claim that contributory social security can only function under conditions of steady economic growth (that is, of rising real income), a claim that is a somewhat exaggerated interpretation of public reaction to tolerable fluctuations that could not immediately be absolved by adequately financed reserve funds.

Increasing contribution rates is inherent in the maturation process of the pay-as-you-go system. To mitigate the financial burden on future generations, contributions higher than necessary to cover current benefits are set from the start in the early years of the program. This permits the buildup of a reserve fund and the payment of some benefits to those generations who cannot qualify for the full pension due to their age and who, in recognition of past service, receive payments not covered by their contributions. This financing system requires forecasts of future benefit expenditures and rising contribution rates to cover them up to and beyond maturation.

Add to this the fear that future income will not meet future prices. It is forecasts of increased future pension expenses that may create the apprehension on the part of the present labor force that future contribution rates may be intolerably high. Uncertain whether their own retirement income is assured—that is, whether future generations will be able or will want to support the pensions of present contributors—workers may resent escalating taxes. This could lead to the termination of the unwritten intergenerational contract and a weakening of the solidarity between currently active and retired workers.

If the glum economic predictions for the Western world require a reduction in the standard of living of the entire population, the retired must shoulder their share. A situation, as reported by the Swedes, where the real income of pensioners is to increase by 4.3 percent annually through 1983, while that of the economically active is expected to increase by only 1.3 percent per year, is untenable in the long run. Between 1968 and 1978, the income of German pensioners—whose public pension is tax free—rose by 45 percent; that of the taxpayer increased by only 35 percent. Pensioners cannot expect an unintended shift of the distribution of income in their favor without a strong reaction from the contributors. These considerations underlie the demand for a full-fledged review of the social security system, now underway in some of the European countries as well as in the United States. Current and potential misgivings of contributors, which were expressed in nearly all the European papers, have to be seen against the background of the high level of total social security contributions already being paid. In Denmark, Sweden, and France, the combined tax load already approaches 50 percent of payroll. In 1978, the tax load represented more than 43 percent of the French gross national product. Past experience shows that workers and employers have good reasons to fear substantial increases in the size of contributions. Contribution rates have increased over time in most countries.[3] Furthermore, indirect taxes like the value-added tax (VAT) and inflation sap the purchasing power of the reduced take home pay.

Hence, social security faces: (1) the current dismal prospect for increased real income, due to low employment, slow economic growth, and the need for increased expenditures for energy imports in the foreseeable future; (2) the worldwide inability to come to grips with inflation, whereby wages in most of the countries lag not only in time, but also in extent, behind prices; (3) the expected further dislocation of jobs, made necessary by the need to restructure and reequip the economy (in turn required by the need for improved productivity and the growing competition by the Third World in technologically less advanced industrial products); and (4) the recently experienced effects of the first and second oil shock upon social security reserve funds. Thus, the demand for (increased) government support of the social security system becomes understandable.

GENERAL REVENUE SUPPORT

The universal (folk) part of the Danish pension system is financed in full by general revenues. The Swedish government makes up any deficit that employer contributions to the universal and earnings-related pension program leave uncovered. In 1974 these amounted to 30.7 percent of the total receipts of these two tiers of the public program. The German social insurance pension system has been subsidized in increasing amounts, but at a reducing rate by the government, which has acknowledged a moral obligation to cover any deficit. The 1979–1980 rate of 16 percent is likely to be reduced to support the unemployment compensation system (*Die Quelle,* December 1980, p. 671).

The United States government makes only very small contributions to specific insignificant parts of the pension expenses, but—in the view of most observers—assumes the same moral obligation. Where, as in Germany and Sweden, there are separate administrations of pensions for manual and white-collar workers, and where one of them (that covering manual workers as a rule) experiences a loss of contributors and revenues while the other prospers, a transfer of resources is obligatory. France has taken the concept of the indivisibility of social insurance protection a step further by requiring those branches of social security that enjoy surpluses to finance deficits in others. The income of the Family Allowance Program for many years exceeded expenditures. This surplus (accumulated reserves) was siphoned off to finance deficits in old-age pension and health insurance programs. In both Germany and France, some of the "special" systems covering declining industries (such as agriculture and mining) require government financial support. The French government, as many others, underwrites the recurrent deficits in the "special programs," predominantly in declining industries and occupations (such as railroads or mining). It also shouldered the employer contribution in certain economically disadvantaged regions. Several of the more than 120 French special schemes receive central government subsidies ranging from 7.4 to 26.6 percent, resulting in a total governmental contribution of 13.5 percent of total receipts.

In none of these countries has the demand for general revenue support produced such a heated level of controversy as in the United States, where even labor—largely out of fear of the unavoidable politicization of the whole program—opposes a *major* shift toward government financing. All of the countries hesitate to rely upon further expansion of public expenditures, regardless of the way they would be financed. Nowhere is this clearer than in the United Kingdom, where the Conservative government aims to load onto employers one part of the public social expenditures, the first eight weeks of cash sickness benefits, by 1984.

EXPENDITURE REDUCTIONS

To gear up for the need to meet the effects of the present and, in particular, the future increased pension load upon social security finances, some of the countries seek to reduce pension benefits. Obviously, a decrease of the current, nominal amounts is politically difficult to achieve. It would further destroy the social myth and may lead to substantial resistance to the payments of the payroll tax. The target therefore shifts to a reduction of future benefit growth, either by a change in the benefit formula reducing the replacement value, or by reducing the extent of adjustment to price- or wage-level changes.

The Federal Republic of Germany has used both approaches as temporary measures to improve the current financial base of its contingency reserve. Since 1978, pension adjustments to price- and wage-level changes, whichever are higher, have not been computed on gross, but on net (after-tax) earnings. They were cancelled for 1978, were "capped" at 4.5 percent for 1979, and at 4 percent for the following year. Observers of the German system will remember that an earlier (1957) elimination of adjustment produced a lasting reduction of the replacement rate. A similar result was reached by design in the 1977 changes in the benefit formula in the United States, which canceled an unintended increase in the replacement value resulting from previous amendments.

In the United Kingdom under the present Conservative government, the main short-term benefit change proposed involves the phasing out of earnings-related supplements to the basic flat-rate benefits. As an interim measure, a temporary cut of 5 percent was imposed pending legislation to bring short-term benefits (flat-rate unemployment compensation, cash sick pay, and disability benefits) under income taxation. The insured in the United Kingdom also lost the adjustment to wage-level changes, which was replaced by an adjustment to price level only.

CHANGES TO CAPITAL FUNDING

None of the five European countries seeks to replace or to supplement the current pay-as-you-go system of financing pensions by capital funding. This attitude is firmly held in spite of a growing literature that attacks pay-as-you-go financing as weakening the propensity to save, hence starving the capital market. An Organization for Economic Cooperation and Development (OECD) report (1980) defined the intergenerational transfer which underlies current financing as "each generation being spared the worry of having to accumulate reserves of their own." Evidence as to the effect of current financing of pensions upon the volume of private savings is conflicting. More recent studies believe the effect to be of manageable proportions. West Germany, France, and some of the other countries are influenced by past experiences with the effects of war-induced inflation upon such funds. The older German system (1886) saw them dissipated in the runaway inflation following World War I, and both France and Germany saw these funds disappear again after World War II, requiring the establishment of new programs based upon current financing.

This difficulty could be overcome by investing such funds into indexed instruments of indebtedness, if available. The British "Granny" bonds, available at present to individuals at pension age and, in modest quantities, to pension funds, are of this nature. It is doubtful, however, that any government would be willing to issue such bonds in the necessary quantity, which would mean shouldering unconditionally the total risk of inflation for the swelling capital funds. Nor would it be easy in contributory systems to raise the premium (payroll taxes) sufficiently to accumulate such funds, given the present and future high level of the contribution burden and the growing distrust of government's future ability and willingness to live up to its pension promises.[4]

The effect of sufficiently large capital accumulation (which would be needed to produce an income that could finance future benefits in full or in large part) upon the supply of capital for the private sector and upon the interest rate, is not known, but it is feared to be substantial. To invest the funds in private securities and bonds would add the risk of default to that of inflation, and would possibly impair the program's ability to serve its main function of maintaining the income of the aged. It requires managerial skills not easily and cheaply available in the administration of public or quasi-public agencies. The investment of large social security capital funds in indexed government bonds may affect the central bank's ability to manage the national money and credit supply unless these indexed securities are held in a compartmentalized isolated status.[5] Their very existence may generate a demand for widespread issue of indexed bonds, leaving the government to carry a risk largely beyond its control.

DUAL-PURPOSE CAPITAL FUNDING

There are two examples of the use of the social security payroll tax for the accumulation of capital funds: Sweden and Denmark. In an imaginative trade-off of pensions for wage increases, Danish unions agreed to forego wage hikes for two years in return for a work-time-determined[6] higher retirement pay from a government contribution to the second-tier pension fund. There the government contribution is kept in an "Employees Special Pension Fund." Eighty percent of this fund must be invested in bonds, housing, loans to municipalities, or producer and consumer cooperatives. An unusual feature of this arrangement consists of the provision that 20 percent can be invested in the equity market, with the proviso that no more than 20 percent of the shares in any one company can be acquired. This permits the board of directors of this special fund, which is dominated by unions (employers are excluded), to contribute within its modest means to the revival of the Danish industry, in particular to the export-oriented branches in the advanced-technology field. This part of the Employee Special Pension Fund is exempt from the policy governing the investment of the reserve fund accumulated in the Danish work-time-related second layer, which must "ensure adequate security, maintenance of the actual value of the funds, and the highest possible yields" (Gutchess, 1980b, p. 9). A similar investment policy governs the Danish third-tier private pension fund. A government proposal to extend the principle of channeling parts of pension funds into risk investment to shore up wilting business enterprises is pending.

The Danish capital funds are small. They were the result of a one-time agreement; hence, their revenues are unlikely to reduce greatly future contribution rates to the work-time-related pension programs, or to increase substantially these benefits. Still, the latter were increased in 1980 by 16 percent. This is not true for the much larger and older Swedish Capital Fund, established under the employer-financed, wage-related second-tier pension program. The return on the investments of this fund are credited with having covered the cost of all of the annual earnings-related pension expenditures of the social security system between 1960 and 1975. Lowering of the retirement age from 67 to 65, which increased the pension volume as well as the erosion of the value of capital due to inflation, lowered the real return rate of that fund's investment so that benefit outgo exceeded the return. Like the Danish pension funds, the purpose of the Swedish capital fund was initially twofold. It was to serve not merely as a means of avoiding large increases in contributions when the program matures after 1990, but also as a way of increasing aggregate savings as a basis for a higher rate of investment. The Swedish National Pension Fund benefited from the large excess of employer contributions over pension expenditures in the early years of the earnings-related second tier of the Swedish social insurance pension program, established 20 years ago. As this excess diminished, the accumulation rate had to fall. As Spant (1981) reported, past conservative long-term investment offering only low returns now endangers the ability of this fund to serve its main purpose (the financing of wage-related pensions) unless the second-tier earnings-related pension shifts to pay-as-you-go financing in the future.

Still, until recently it was the major source of capital formation, equaling almost 17 times the annual expenditures of the earnings-related pension program in 1978. This percentage is falling by design. Its three subdivisions (one fund for public employees and employees in companies in which the government has a controlling influence, the second fund for employees in enterprises with more than 20 wage earners, and the third one for employees in small firms) invested in good securities at good interest rates, readily redeemable, but offering low returns. Most of them are government bonds and housing loans (72 percent) and loans to mostly industrial enterprises (10 percent). The latter were made to contributing firms up to an amount equaling 50 percent of the individual firm's previous year's contributions (retroverse loans). About 1 percent of the total fund's assets, accumulated in a fourth fund, can be committed, with parliamentary approval, in the stock market.

This type of investment serves the same purpose as that made by the 20 percent portion of the Danish Employee Special Pension Fund. It is an investment fund designed to stimulate the Swedish capital market, to increase the supply of risk capital, and to invest in production, thereby creating new jobs. The investments have to be made with due regard for their safety, adequate return, and satisfactory liquidity. Certain restrictions are placed on the choice of investments in specific types of industries and the percentage of total shares outstanding that the fourth fund is allowed to own in each company. Its returns are taxable. Unlike the three major subdivisions, it does not pay out pensions.

It is significant to note that both systems use only a small part of the pension funds to assist the country with revamping its economic structure in pursuit of greater productivity and a stronger competitive international trade position. These goals were, however, supported by the unions in the hope that this investment in new industries would provide new jobs for their members. The largest part of the capital accumulations was to serve the main purpose of reducing future contributions to the state pension programs. As mentioned above, the efficacy of this function is now in question, due to the effect of inflation and the poor return on past investments.

EARLY RETIREMENT REVISITED

One of the major drains on social security pension programs and on the labor force has been mentioned previously, namely, the general early retirement option. The reversal of retirement trends and early claims to pension benefits is indeed one of the more promising, but long-range, measures for the improvement of the financial position of public and private pension programs.

Early and flexible retirement is generally considered the result of an irreversible trend, at least for now. Some co-researchers note that some applications of the early retirement device respond to generally accepted social needs. The governments' attitudes toward a generally available early retirement option, offering a higher pension than the actuarially reduced one to all insured, are quite reserved. The popularity of early retirement notwithstanding, the justification for offering general early retirement is somehow vague and is based upon such hard-to-prove factors as the increased speed of technological change, the greater physical and psychological requirements of work, and the increased danger to health and safety that leads to reduced ability to work at upper ages. These factors may be quantifiable in special cases.

Early retirement of workers in arduous, hazardous, and unhealthy employment falls into the first category of special cases. The physically and mentally disabled and the handicapped, and others suffering from premature exhaustion close to pensionable age, but not yet entitled to a disability benefit under the strict definitions of the invalidity law, are also preferred. So are persons in the 60–64 age group who have been unemployed[7] for a protracted period within a somewhat longer spell of time and who can no longer claim unemployment benefits (Sweden, Germany). In these contingencies, early retirement can hardly be denied, for humanitarian and economic reasons. Nor can early retirement before "normal pensionable age" be questioned for workers with long years of service (France, Germany). They must be presumed to have made their contributions to society and to have paid their share of the cost of their social security benefits. If there is such a thing as a "right to leisure" late in life (for example, after age 60), these people have earned it.

All this should not be confused with the trend toward offering early retirement to all workers. Such a generally available option is being sought in two ways: (1) by easing the conditions under which early retirement is currently granted, for instance, by considering any age beyond 45 as disabling the worker for obtaining a new job or retraining for the old one; or (2) by insisting on lowering the "normal pensionable age" itself (proposed in West Germany). In the United Kingdom, this demand takes the form of seeking equalization of the male and the female retirement ages. Equalization implies lowering the male retirement age to the female level of 60, or setting the age between 60 and 65. As we have pointed out previously, unions are exerting pressure for an eventual reduction to age 60 in retirement age for men. There is also a separate demand for selective reduction in arduous occupations in the United Kingdom. (Mine workers have already achieved this.)

In some countries, general early retirement is supported by the social partners—labor and management—and by a few government officials as a way to relieve unemployment, particularly that of the younger workers. This is the rationale of the English Job Release Scheme, the French Premature Retirement Benefit Laws, and the Danish severance pay program. The validity of this argument has been questioned, however. French and German experience shows that very few vacated jobs are filled by the young or other unemployed. This view is shared by the Danish unions and employers. About one-half of the vacancies created by early retirement are not filled at all, but disappear in the reorganization of the production process (capital substitution). Nor are the younger workers always equipped by training and work experience to fill the vacancies of the early retirees. At best, a few of the unemployed are admitted to the lower rungs of the career ladder, if older workers who stay employed move up to fill the job openings. In many cases, the use of the early retirement option is not a voluntary act of the worker, but the result of management pressure to lower labor costs, to avoid severance pay, and to reduce fringe benefits.

Such early retirement provisions, whether enshrined in the old-age or the disability pension or in unemployment compensation programs, liberalize the age conditions of income-maintenance programs for the elderly. These are, however, long-term programs, necessarily concerned with the long-term financing of current and future benefits. On the other hand, the problem of youth unemployment is a short-term problem susceptible to a variety of remedial manpower measures. It is questionable whether the need for maintaining a constant and dependable long-term program could and should be sacrificed through frequent changes of its main provisions in line with changing short-term objectives of labor market policy.

Converting a long-term income-maintenance program into a tool of labor market policy (dual-purpose law) could destroy public support for the public pension, which demands stability and continuity of its main provisions. The need for dependable continuity of long-term pension programs would make it as difficult to use social security to reverse the early retirement option tomorrow, when a shortage of young workers requires workers between 60 and 65 to remain on their jobs, as it would be to reinstate it under opposite conditions. Nor are the mainstays of the social security system, such as the size of the benefit or contribution, proper tools of a contracyclical (constantly changing, short-term) economic program. When Lord Keynes first suggested this to Arthur Altmeyer, the first administrator of the United States Social Security System, Altmeyer rejected this dual-purpose program because he feared that it would endanger the ability of the social security program to offer constant protection to the nation at predictable costs, contributions, and benefits.[8]

Early retirement statutes for special cases, such as older workers unable to find employment, are often implemented in a way that makes them generally available to insured workers other than those they are designed to cover, even if the other groups do not meet all the qualifications of the law. Often the definitions governing the contingency and qualifications for the receipt of an early retirement pension are—probably by design—drawn so widely or so interpreted as to allow nearly all claimants a full (that is, not actuarially or otherwise reduced) pension. France and Sweden are examples of this. The Swedish worker can retire at age 60 with a full pension, even if that worker is less than half disabled. Poor labor market conditions, which offer the worker little or no prospects of employment, are held to constitute a disability. For many years, France used the disability program to equip the aged between 60 and 64 with a pension, basically by equating old age itself with disability.

FLEXIBLE RETIREMENT

Flexible pensions, which allow the qualified German claimant with 35 years of contributions to retire and draw a pension anytime between ages 63 and

67, have been hailed as a great social achievement, since they give the insured worker the freedom to determine unilaterally the upper limit of his or her work life. In spite of fairly generous inducements to work beyond age 63, the result has been for German workers to retire at the earliest possible moment, 63. The upper limit (67) of flexibility has rarely been used. For all practical purposes, flexible retirement has mostly changed into early retirement for long-service workers.

The right to shape the final years of one's working life has been carried the furthest in Sweden. Quite apart from the partial pension law, discussed subsequently, the Swedish insured worker can choose to (1) retire with a full pension at age 65; (2) continue working beyond that age until age 70 with an increased pension; (3) retire between 60 and 64 at a reduced pension (0.5 percent per month); (4) draw in the same period a half pension while still earning additional pension credits; (5) interrupt, between 60 and 70, the receipt of the pension as often as desired and choose between full and half pension; or (6) take advantage of the partial pension program, which in some aspects falls outside the retirement pay program proper. Partially disabled or prematurely aged and long-term unemployed workers may retire at a full pension five years before age 65.

SWEDEN'S PARTIAL PENSION PROGRAM

The Swedish partial pension program has stirred the imagination of the social security planners in the whole world. It is indeed a new device promoting partial retirement, which does not merely leave the retirement pension claim proper intact, but increases it. Workers and the self-employed earn pension credits both on partial work wages and on partial reimbursement for foregone earnings, thereby increasing the retirement pension to which a worker is entitled at age 65. The Partial Pension Insurance Act of 1975, as amended in 1979, is designed to encourage a reduction in work activity (originally made possible by an influx of young foreign workers) on the part of insured workers between the ages of 60 and 64 who (1) had earned 10 years of credits under the (second) earnings-related government pension layer after age 45, (2) were employed for at least 5 out of the last 12 months, and (3) had worked at least 22 hours per week immediately before making a claim.

Originally, if the worker reduced weekly working hours by at least 5 hours, to not less than 17 hours of paid employment, the government undertook to replace 65 percent of the wage loss—without reducing the size of the regular earnings-related pension available at age 65. However, as of January 1, 1981, the compensation level was reduced to 50 percent. This reduction was a response to the growing cost of this very popular program.[9]

The shift to part-time employment results in lower earnings from work and also a part-time pension that, at least until January 1981, left the worker with 85 to 90 percent of his previous income.[10] (A similar result is expected for the self-employed who have to reduce their work by at least 50 percent.) There is, of course, the danger that this measure—which was designed to prepare the worker for full retirement—would be used by employers to pressure workers to apply for part-time work instead of full employment in the enterprise. There is some evidence that this occurred in a substantial number of the cases (some 25 percent).

Nevertheless, the partial pension program can be viewed as a form of flexible retirement, increasing both the worker's and the consenting employer's choice of how to reduce the work obligation in the five years before final retirement at a minimum loss of income, if partial jobs in or (rarely) outside the previous employment can be located. It could also be regarded as a form of early (gradual) retirement. To some extent, it can be viewed as similar to a pension, as indicated by its way of financing through a surcharge upon the employer's contribution to the earnings-related government pension. Due to its very generous payments, it has practically rendered other Swedish provisions for early retirement inoperative. The very generosity also reduced the chance of its being copied, unchanged, in the rest of the more cost-conscious industrialized countries at this time, which feel less able to fund such a scheme. In Sweden, the partial pension program has been a great success. As indicated before, about one-quarter of the eligible persons had taken advantage of its provisions by 1980, forcing the government to double the surcharge on the employers' contributions to the earnings-related pension scheme.

SUMMARY

The social security pension systems in the five European countries, as in the United States, encounter serious financial problems due, in part, to a worsening of the ratio of contributors to pensioners and to the increased benefit level. Inflation is the main factor affecting the latter; unemployment is one of the elements in the reduction of revenues. Both may be of a temporary nature and subject to government policy outside the social security system. Aging of the population is most likely the single major factor that will affect the size of benefit expenditures in the future. This would also hold true if the pensions were not further liberalized—an unrealistic assumption, given the pressure of powerful political groups to improve the pension rights of women and to reduce further the normal pensionable retirement age. The financial situation of the social security systems will be further endangered if the change in the demand for labor, prevailing low fertility rates, and employment of foreign workers reduce the manpower supply available for the contributing active labor force.

None of the remedies to be taken by the social security pension programs that have been discussed or implemented so far promises to close the future gap between revenues and expenditures after the year 2000, although they may offer temporary relief. All of them face powerful opposition, be it increased contribution rates, government subsidies, or lowering of benefits or capital funding. Some others, like increased coverage (for women and immigrants, for example), cannot permanently improve the financial position of the social security system. The trend toward early retirement is still so pervasive that only a dire necessity such as a wartime shortage of labor or a runaway inflation can be relied upon to reverse this trend. The expectation in some European countries that low fertility may cause labor shortages by 1990 or early in the twenty-first century depends upon too many uncertainties outside the social security system to serve as a solid basis for social policy.

In the following chapters, two types of remedies will be discussed which, if their problems can be solved, can be expected over time to ease the income requirements of an aging society: (1) a shift from predominant reliance upon the social security pensions to other income-maintenance mechanisms, and (2) the improvement of earnings opportunities for the elderly by prolonging their working life—which, in turn, would relieve the expenditure load of government and private pensions.

7

Shifting Some of the Burden to the Private Sector

Views differ on the proper function of the public pension programs. Historically, public pensions were intended to provide only basic income needs of the insured. It was thus left to the insured and/or employers to complement the statutory benefit through private pension plans and invested savings to achieve the desired level of protection. This view applies to both the Bismarckian and the Beveridge types of system.[1] In the prosperous 1950s and 1960s, workers whose standard of living had increased looked first to the public pension program for higher benefits, that is, to public benefits providing a higher percentage of their pre-retirement earnings. However, an improved pension which better met basic needs still had to be supplemented by one which stressed equity even more, one that more fully reflected the increased level of contributions and past earnings.

Some controversy about the meaning of basic protection has always existed. Neither the earnings-related pension nor the universal pension, as it was first installed, provided for basic needs, however they were defined. Nor was there a general agreement over what percentage of the pre-retirement income was necessary to cover basic needs, much less to maintain the living standards of the elderly. Protection of the retiree's financial need grew as a result of political pressure and was made possible by economic growth. Goals, such as matching the replacement rate for government officials, as in Germany, were never based upon an analysis of whether the 75 percent rate achieved in the government's pension plans covered or exceeded the retired government worker's needs. Nor was full legislative recognition ever given to the efforts of Sir William Beveridge's and Pierre Laroque's commission reports relating "basic" needs to a food, clothing, and shelter requirement.

The economic progress and the political climate of the three decades following the end of World War II led to promises of relatively high public pensions in all five European countries, often achieved by adding additional pension layers upon each other. This resulted in claims that rather high rates of replacement would be achieved when the pension system matured, normally within 20 to 30 years. In the interim, the systems produced far lower rates (see Chapter 5, table 5.6). A series of changes of the law (as in the United Kingdom) and of later liberalization measures with later maturation dates constantly postponed the time when the insured individual could hope to see the promises of gratifying benefits fulfilled.

The gap between the replacement value of the public pension and the perceived need of the retiree has been filled in various degrees by private pensions in some of the five countries. On the average, about 50 percent of the wage and salaried workers with at least average earnings are covered by their employers, often with the assistance of private insurance in a variety of pension arrangements. This produces retirement benefits that complement the public pensions and increase retirement income. Such plans protect 66 percent of the workers in Germany and 75 percent of the male and 62 percent of the female workers over 25 in the United Kingdom (25 percent of the total work force). In contrast, only 4 percent of the manual workers and 25 percent of the salaried workers are covered by private pensions in Denmark.

Private pensions historically preceded public pensions. Where they existed in great number and strength, they were built into the public scheme. This is the case in the United Kingdom, where the second-tier earnings-related part of the pension can be "contracted out" to private providers if they meet certain minimum requirements.[2] Other interrelationships include limiting private pension coverage to that part of the earnings not covered by state pensions (France and Sweden), or reducing the private pension by the state pension (United States and, formerly, Germany). Conceived as an addition to the public pension, private pension benefits are as a rule relatively small. Most of them amount to a fraction of the social security pension and add at best only 15 to 20 percent to the latter's replacement ratio. In the United Kingdom, the well-developed private pensions replace, on the average, 16.7 percent of pre-retirement income.

Interest in private pension systems grew in several of the European countries for a variety of reasons. In Sweden, a highly unionized country, it stemmed from the union's perception that the universal system, together with the work-related system, still yielded fairly low retirement benefits. Good industrial relations prevailing at the time in that country permitted the creation of a third layer of private pension arrangement, binding for the members of the national organizations of employers and labor. In France, the ceiling on contributions and benefits in the pattern-setting[3] general scheme was kept so low as to leave a large part of the income of the higher-paid professional and managerial workers free from contribution and, in consequence, disregarded in the computation of the basic public pension. Their union (CGC) succeeded in establishing private pension programs on top of the general scheme; these provided pensions based upon contributions on the excess of earnings over the ceiling in the public system. The several pension funds of that type formed an umbrella organization (AGIRC). Other parts of the labor force followed this example, and their pension plans federated in another central body (ARRCO). The government later extended those schemes to all enterprises, regardless of affiliation to the original bargaining organizations in the covered industries.

Germany offers examples of a different type. Here, management's desire to improve the loyalty of the work force to the firm, and to hold on to a well-trained, often highly skilled work force, prompted it to tie the personnel to the enterprise by a pension plan that offered nontransferable pension rights.

A small number of pension plans for high-level managerial personnel, originally stemming from feudalistic and paternalistic impulses, exists in all five countries. Where strong unions occasionally forego large wage increases, as in Germany and Denmark, private pensions—deferred wages—may offer a trade-off against wage increases, as it did in the United States during the wage freeze of World War II. Private pension plans also grow if the public pension is inadequate or is rendered so through lagging adjustment to cost-of-living increases for a protracted period of time.

As private pension funds grow, so grows the unions' interest in gaining some influence over the investment policies of their large capital accumulations. In 1980 the British pension funds and life assurance companies owned one-third of the securities listed on the stock exchange. By the year 2000, this ratio is expected to double. In 1979 their combined inflow of new funds was in the range of £9 billion to £10 billion. More than one-half emanated from the pension funds, fed by premiums paid in by union members or paid on their behalf (Davies, 1981).

PRIVATE PENSIONS AS SUBSTITUTES FOR PUBLIC PENSIONS

Current interest in private pensions has been heightened by the fight against inflation, which, in the United Kingdom and the United States, centers at present upon a reduction of public expenditures. Such a policy leads to the shifting of public functions to the private sector. In the United Kingdom, "contracting out" of occupational pensions to private reinsured employer funds is therefore encouraged by tax advantages not available to the worker who stays in the state pension program.[4] Shifting the task of maintaining the income of the retired to the employers and their pension funds, and away from payroll taxes, may avoid the contributors' aversion to taxes. This may make the plan more acceptable to insured workers, as long as they do not realize the cost of such a move (such as the effect on wages and consumer budgets).

PRIVATE PENSIONS AND SAVINGS

Another impetus for greater reliance upon private pensions derives from the widespread view held by many economists, and shared by management, that the capital needed for retooling industry to improve productivity and economic growth is in short supply, and that it could be found in privately administered pension plans,[5] but not in the currently financed pension program. This view, supported strongly by the private insurance industry, points to the fact that contractual private pension obligations must be fully funded in order to enable the insurer to honor all outstanding claims when they become due. Unlike the compulsory public system, which can afford to operate on the pay-as-you-go principle, the private insurer has no guarantee of future insured workers whose premiums can be relied upon to cover pension expenditures. To avoid increasing premiums, these funds must be invested. The controversial view holds that they represent a large share of private savings, one of the major and preferred sources of capital available for investment. Opponents point to the fact that pension funds are not as a rule invested in new ventures, but predominantly in already listed securities. They also argue that private pensions reduce private savings—the source of new investment—to a significant degree. Although opinions differ on the extent to which reliance on public pensions reduces the level of individuals' savings, some reduction of aggregate private savings is likely to occur, enough to attract the interest of some economists in expanding the role of private pensions in the income-maintenance program of the elderly.

Not all private pension plans accumulate investment funds. Some were—and some still are—unsecured bookkeeping entries in the employer's books (self insurance), not set aside and invested. Hence, the pension payments depend upon the employer's ability to pay and his liquidity at the time the pension falls due. Such arrangements do not require the separation of funds from working capital. This practice has been banned by law and by regulations in the United Kingdom and Sweden, and in the United States where, in addition, the enterprises have to insure their pension funds with government-sponsored or regulated insurance companies.

Large-scale funds are not accumulated in the French private pension field. Although originating in nationwide collective bargaining, government extension of pensions to all employment has made them compulsory. This permits current (pay-as-you-go) financing, administered by the two umbrella organizations (AGIRC and ARRCO), and others, which in turn does not require full capital funding. The relatively small reserve (contingency) trust funds are not significant sources of investment capital in that country.

VESTING IN PRIVATE PENSIONS

The problem of vesting has, in principle, been solved. The United Kingdom (contracted-out pensions), West Germany, and Sweden, like the United States, protect workers who leave their job before retirement against the loss of the pension credits acquired up to the date of departure. This applies to workers after a minimum age, with a minimum number of years of service ranging from 1 to 15 and affiliation for a minimum period in the private pension fund (0–2 years). In some cases, the worker's right to join the fund is automatically granted with the start of employment. In other cases, it is guaranteed after a probationary period (1–2 years).

TRANSFER OF VESTED PENSION CREDITS

Portability, or the right to carry accumulated pension credits to the next employer or employers, ultimately requires a transfer of funds between the pension funds of two or more employers. As such, it constitutes a more difficult problem. Like vesting, portability is assured in the public pension system. This feature, together with indexing, is one of the main reasons for union preference for the state pension system. Employer preference for private pensions, however, stems largely from personnel management advantages as seen in more flexible, tailor-made arrangements and in increased loyalty. In Sweden, where all members of the national employer association and all national unions that are parties to the nationwide collective bargaining agreement are insured by the two insurance carriers for manual and salaried workers, portability within the two insurance communities (but not between them) is available. A similar result is reached by the two French umbrella organizations of technical, professional, and managerial employees in AGIRC, and others in ARRCO. No such mechanisms exist on a nationwide scale in Germany, the United Kingdom, or the United States (with the exception of a rather complicated procedure in the United Kingdom for the transfer of a limited part of the vested pension credits to the government program to protect guaranteed minimum pensions). Within the public sector in the United Kingdom, a transfer to other public sector schemes on a year-for-year basis or with little loss of pension rights is possible in most public sector occupations.

PROTECTING PRIVATE PENSIONS AGAINST INFLATION

The most intractable problem facing the privately insured worker is the inflation-proofing of vested credits and, more importantly, of the pension itself. Some of the adjustment of benefits to wage or price changes is achieved via the distribution of the pay-as-you-go income in France, and of "surpluses" in Sweden, but not necessarily to the extent offered by the automatic adjustment process of the respective public systems. In other words, they do not pay as much. Voluntary ad hoc adjustments, depending upon the profitability and liquidity of the firm, often prove inadequate and limit the adjustment to a low percentage that is outpaced by inflation. In the United Kingdom, the better private pension plans covered an average of only 60 percent of the price increase between 1972 and 1977. (Some were fully indexed, and some not at all.) Laws and court decisions in West Germany force the employer to review the adequacy of the private pension every three years, and, if necessary, to increase benefits to cover at least one-half of the increase in the cost-of-living index. This is not the case in the United States. In the United Kingdom, the guaranteed minimum pension (GMP), which is equivalent to the social security earnings-related pension, is protected. According to Fogarty, anything above the GMP is protected only in the sense that it must be related to wage and salary at the date of leaving.

In this partial guarantee there lies, in embryonic form, a possible but costly solution to the problem caused by the inability of the private pension system to assure the beneficiary of the full value of his or her retirement pay. This inability arises from the fact that because of the full funding principle, the private pension is tied to an actuarially determined ratio of premiums to pension, which in turn puts before the actuary the impossible task of estimating the costs of inflation in the future. This also places an unknown cost burden upon the enterprise. The United Kingdom solution transfers this risk for a part of the occupational pension to the state. Purists may find this solution wanting, if applied to the total pension volume, since it compels the state to bail out a private system over which the government has only general supervision.[6] Political economists are likely to object to loading the cost of the inflation guarantee on all taxpayers, whether insured or not. (Another solution, the issue of indexed bonds, has been discussed in chapter 5 with regard to capital funding and the reservations applying to this device.)

PROTECTION OF PRIVATE
PENSIONS AGAINST DEFAULT

Assuring the employers' ability to fulfill the pension promise requires reinsurance. While vesting is enforced by state law, portability can best be achieved by a nationwide organization of all private pension plans with near uniform programs. The same holds true for nationwide reinsurance and for even partial inflation-proofing. All these problems are more easily solved, and at less cost, by a nationwide government social security program that also offers beneficiaries the security of the nation's credit backing up pension promises. The government pension can also fully safeguard the purchasing power (and, if desired, the relation of pension to current wages).

THE COST OF PRIVATE INSURANCE

The costs to the insured of a private pension unit, and the total costs of retirement pay to the economy, may be higher than those arising in a national government pension program. This is because the administrative costs of private pensions are likely to exceed those of a state system. Economy of size would be lost if the system is Balkanized into thousands of employer plans. Both the number of administrators and the number of government supervisors would increase.

A NATIONWIDE NETWORK OF PRIVATE PENSIONS

As the French experience shows, a nationwide private pension, if made compulsory by law, can also use the pay-as-you-go method of financing. The Swedish and French examples prove the need for the creation of one or more nationwide umbrella organizations to emulate the state pension program's unique ability to equalize the load between strong and weak pension funds and to assure portability (and provide indexing) on a uniform basis. For this purpose, these organizations must be equipped with some enforcement powers provided by their own statutes or by the state. The national organizations themselves remain subject to state regulations, as do their members. If, therefore, an economy decides to replace or to supplement the state pension by a private pension system, compulsory membership in a national umbrella association becomes necessary to safeguard the interests of the insured workers. This is made quite clear in the British report, which advocates this course of action for the contracted-out occupational pensions, unless the body politic decides to replace the latter with the government's program. Should this happen, the remaining private pensions would remain voluntary mechanisms, solely responsible for pension supplement, without any safeguards for transferability and inflation-proofing of pensions.

SAVINGS

The need to increase the revenues or to reduce the benefit level of public pension programs would be less if more of the aged population could fall back on savings and investment income to supplement their pensions. A similar result could be achieved by reducing out-of-pocket expenses of the aged. This is being done in nearly all European countries and the United States through national and local tax privileges; reduced transportation costs; easy access to higher education and entertainment; cheaper housing, rent, and utilities; subsidies; and many other concessions, most of them means-tested devices.

Private Savings

State, and sometimes employer, subsidies encourage workers to set aside regularly a certain sum or a percentage of earnings in order to induce a savings habit that would yield accumulated returns available after retirement. Alternatively, such savings could assist in the acquisition of assets, such as life insurance or a house, which would save rental expenditures or serve as a possible source of income.

The French government emphasized compulsory capital formation and profit sharing. The German government matches a worker's savings up to a certain amount if it is either held for five years or invested in housing. The latter objective is also served by concessionary interest rates and real property taxes. Between 1957 and 1971, Denmark established price-indexed savings contracts for age groups 18–56 and offered tax concessions for private savings and the earnings thereon. The inflation risk was covered by the government. The United Kingdom offers tax-free savings, tax incentives for employee-acquired profit-sharing stocks, and index-linked retirement certificates. Fear of inflation robbed most savings efforts of their attraction, and profit sharing in the form of stock ownership yielded only insignificant and uncertain equity. Tax deferment, as under the Keogh and Individual Retirement Account systems in the United States, is being studied in the five countries. Many of these measures are based upon an ideology that aims to give workers (and in Sweden, the union) a stake in economic wealth. Some, like profit sharing, also intend to heighten the worker's identification with the enterprise and thereby increase productivity. They seek to tie the worker firmly to the existing economic system and to reduce excessive mobility.

Up to the present, these measures have had only limited effect. More importantly, due to the heavily skewed distribution of income within the aged group, such measures benefit only a small number of retirees. Large numbers of the active labor force—those poorly paid and/or with heavy family responsibilities—are unlikely to be able to take advantage of these programs. Older and better-paid workers may prefer seeking higher retirement income through supplementary private pensions. Lower-paid workers still look to the state pension in preference to means-tested welfare.

Mobilizing Frozen Savings

British and American observers, aware that in these two countries a significant percentage of the aged own their dwellings outright (about one-half and two-thirds, respectively),[7] show considerable interest in mobilizing the savings that these houses represent, by a system of reverse mortgages. Financial institutions are encouraged to lend funds on these assets to the elderly in the expectation that the loan would be repaid by the sale of the property upon the death of the owner. The loan would add to the funds of the elderly and supplement pension receipts. Under the experimental British House Income Plan, the remortgage proceeds are intended to buy an annuity out of which the mortgage interest is also paid. Both this and the U.S. reverse-mortgage scheme are in the pilot stage.

SUMMARY

Up to the present time, neither the private pension, home ownership, nor other forms of investments match individually or together the state pension as a source of cash income of the aged. For example, in Great Britain, where private pensions are well entrenched, 51 percent of the cash income of all households with a retired head came from social security in 1977; 19 percent came from work, 13 percent from private pensions, 10 percent from investments, and 6 percent from home ownership. If the mushrooming of the aged population, a worsening ratio of contributors to beneficiaries, and a growing taxpayer revolt should force greater reliance upon other means of maintaining the income of retired workers, the private-pension option offers a possible solution—if that private pension is nearly universally applied, if it offers workers attractive pensions that can be safeguarded against erosion by inflation, and if nationwide portability can be guaranteed. In EEC countries, portability would have to cover migration among member countries. Once these problems are solved, the difficulties with establishing worldwide portability may be surmountable. A considerable proportion of the aged population would remain unprotected, however. Private insurance does not as a rule cover low-wage, part-time, temporary workers. Homeworkers and persons who are not employed, for example, would also have to look to means-tested welfare or charity for subsistence. The role of savings in any future scheme depends, among other factors, upon changes in the propensity to save and the magnitude of earnings in the future.

8

A Longer Work Life

Delayed retirement would appear to meet some of the current and future problems of social security finances. This would free social security revenues to provide better protection for the growing number of very elderly (75 and older), fill some of the potential gap which a reduced labor force in the future may leave, and meet the employment needs of those older persons (predominantly the "young old") who want and are able to remain in the labor force.

As the previous discussion has implied, work beyond the normal pensionable age (65 and 67 in the countries studied) affects social security finances in two directions: (1) insured workers save the system benefits for the period of employment beyond the conventional retirement age, thus lowering its expenditures (although this may be offset by greater longevity); and (2) in most instances, workers continue to pay social security contributions on their earnings, which increases the system's revenues. Social security systems reward insured workers who delay retirement by offering them higher pensions. These increments, however, which range from a 3 percent to a 10 percent annual increase in benefits expected at normal retirement age (United States and Denmark, respectively), do not always represent a full actuarial increase. Most of the increments are granted only for a five-year period beyond age 65. The West German social security system limits the increment (0.6 percent per month) to two years beyond age 65 for those long-service workers who, under the flexible retirement provisions, are entitled to, but do not use, the early-retirement (63) option. The increments are added to a benefit that, according to the applicable benefit formula, may already have been increased over what the insured could have claimed at normal pensionable age, due to contributions paid on earnings beyond that time. Some of the increments are computed on a weekly basis (United Kingdom, 0.143 percent); others by the month (Germany and Sweden, 0.6 percent; United States, 0.25 percent); on a six-month basis (Denmark, 5 percent); or for a whole year (France, 5 percent).

Regardless of size, the current increments have been reported to have had little effect on the decision to delay retirement, although this may change in the future if high inflation and labor-force shortages prevail. Most private pension systems do not offer any inducements for delayed retirement; some others prohibit it by mandatory retirement provisions.

The European reports prepared for this overview failed to delineate the universe of older workers. The lower age limits vary from age 60 in Denmark, France, and Sweden, to 63 for men and 60 for women in West Germany, and to 64 in the United Kingdom. Some imply that workers who are released at 55 or 56 must also be counted as old in the sense that they require retraining to improve their chances of finding work. Nor is the upper age limit—the age beyond which society no longer expects the elderly to continue working or looking for work—clearly discernible. The statutory "normal" retirement age of 65 or 67 (60 for women in the United Kingdom) cannot necessarily be considered the upper age limit, since most countries provide incentives for delayed retirement. As a rule, these pension increments cease at age 70. The French general scheme seems to go beyond age 70 by maximizing the pension at age 75. Without firm guidance, the following discussion generally refers to 60- to 74-year-olds, with the understanding that most workers between the ages of 60 and 64 encounter fewer employment problems than workers between the ages of 65 and 74.

THE RESERVE ARMY

Since 1973 none of the countries studied has experienced a sharp reduction in the active labor force, and they do not expect to do so before 1990 (Germany) or until the second decade of the next century. Only the future will tell whether the five economies will call on the aged to fill job vacancies not met by a reduced labor force. Obviously, this will also depend upon the size and composition of the labor demand at that time. Until then, the effect of capital substitution on labor demand, and the effect of changes in production techniques on the type and qualifications of labor then in demand, remain speculative. Some prognosticators, basing their forecasts upon the trends of the last 20 years, foresee dramatic shrinkage of the demand for manual and clerical workers through greater use of computerized machines. The simultaneous increase in the demand for trained scientific workers (such as programmers) and the increased need for workers to produce the labor-saving machinery (for example, robots) are not expected to benefit these older workers unless they are retrained and unless public and employer attitudes about their adaptability, learning capacity, and other qualifications undergo marked changes. Nor is there a guarantee that the number of workers that will be required will necessarily match the number of those who have become redundant. Although there may be further growth in the tertiary sector, which up to now offsets the shrinkage in manufacturing and agricultural manpower, the extent of its future growth is unknown. A large part of the growth occurred in public employment (as in Denmark), the primary

target of the fight against inflation and the tax revolt. In the United Kingdom, the tax revolt hits the target indirectly. It centers on taxes and social
security.

Such unpredictable factors hinder any meaningful anticipatory manpower
planning and training action for a contingency which may arise in one or
more decades. While this analysis refers to the mass of the older potential
labor force, it does not exclude the continued employment of highly trained
professionals or cover situations where management encourages older workers to delay retirement because their specific skills, abilities, and experience
cannot be easily replaced through the current labor supply. The labor-force
participation rates for workers 65 and over in the five European countries
and the United States are not likely to reach zero, since some older workers
will inevitably remain employed. Rates could increase as the number of
highly skilled and trained older workers increases, and if biomedical progress is able to slow down the debilitating process associated with aging.

MAGNITUDE OF SUPPLY

Not all workers after age 60 (or even after 45 or 55) are able and willing to
work. If statements of the reason for regular and early retirement given by
retirees in the age groups 60 to 65 or 67 can be believed, about half of the
retirees in the United States retired early for health reasons. Relatively few of
the remaining one-half consider themselves able and willing to accept job
responsibilities (Parnes et al., 1979). A Danish inquiry measuring intentions
to continue working arrived at a figure of 7 to 11 percent (Friis and Hansen,
1980). Similar, but not quantified, attitudes are reported from the United
Kingdom (Fogarty, 1980a). Berglind and Bergroth report that there are
probably very few persons in Sweden who would take advantage of a reform
along the lines of the 1978 amendments to the U.S. Age Discrimination
in Employment Act that raised mandatory retirement age to 70.

In Germany, the government reports that according to a 1980 survey, 75
percent of workers aged 55 intend to retire at 63 (men) and 60 (women). Only
1 out of 10 workers indicated a desire to work beyond 65. Minimal interest in
continued employment among the British, French, Danes, and West Germans was also evident in a 1977 EEC poll, although the total for all EEC
countries reaches 25 percent (Commission of the European Communities,
1978). In sum, there are relatively few elderly who remain eager and available for work beyond the normal pensionable age. This trend is likely to
deepen in the future in the light of the growing concentration of very old
(75-plus) within the aged population.

At present, aging and aged persons who are interested in prolonging their
work life are largely concentrated in the professions, services, and other

white-collar jobs—in general, in occupations that offer job satisfaction that outweighs the desire for leisure and the willingness to accept delayed pension receipt. Other industries with concentrations of older workers are those which offer the workers the prospect for exercising a modicum of independent judgment, those which involve a certain amount of craftsmanship, and industries in sectors that guarantee a measure of security of employment.

Manual workers and those with few skills are more eager to retire, as long as they can count on an adequate retirement pay that is adjusted for inflation. There is a strong correlation between the size (replacement value) of the pension and the change in labor-force participation rates. It seems reasonable to anticipate that the labor-force participation of the older persons and delayed retirement could increase if the size and purchasing power of the nonadjusted or insufficiently adjusted benefit decrease. The need to supplement retirement income may, therefore, be a powerful agent in increasing the proportion of older persons who postpone retirement and seek employment after "regular" retirement.[1] Although this may still be classified as voluntary decision—reducing the standard of living is an alternative—the decision is strongly affected by factors beyond the control of the aged.

OBSTACLES TO EMPLOYMENT BEYOND AGE 65

Age discrimination, layoffs, and, of course, ill health lead to involuntary retirement. The United States is the only country that has raised the lower limit for mandatory retirement in the private sector to a higher level (70) than the normal pensionable age (65). Government prohibition of age discrimination in employment exists in some form in nearly all European countries. As recommended by the ILO, it ends as a rule at age 70. It applies not merely to hiring, transfers, and promotions, but also to access to training. On the other hand, mandatory retirement at pensionable age—a form of age discrimination—exists in many European enterprises. (In France it prevails in the public sector.) In the five European countries, as in any other productivity- and youth-oriented society, there exists an informal type of age discrimination, often based not on an assessment of the specific job requirements compared with the qualifications of the aged job-seeker, but on preconceived notions as to the worker's present and future failings and upon cost considerations. Costs are assumed to be lowered by the greater productivity of the young. In addition, in some of the five European countries, the younger workers command lower wages and have acquired fewer fringe benefits (such as vacations).

As the ILO reports, European research on the strengths and weaknesses of older workers in the countries under study seemed to reach the same conclusions on this subject as research findings in the United States. The five country reports describe few new investigations. In particular, no great effort has gone into the assessment of whether and how biomedical advances have slowed down the aging process. It is hence difficult to reach a conclusion on the progress made up to now, or to project future progress with regard to the additional time span in which the worker over age 60, 65, or 67 may be expected to work beyond the "normal" retirement age. Obviously, few expect the very elderly (75-plus) to work; their increased longevity does, however, lead to increased pension expenditures.

The willingness of the young old to keep working could be measured by efforts made by aging workers who lose their jobs to regain the old job or find a new one, regardless of the availability of the time-limited unemployment compensation or a pre-retirement pension. No data on this subject were submitted by the European co-researchers. Older workers, the European reports state, are not singled out before all others for layoff. This fate is reserved for the young and for women. But once the older workers are unemployed, they remain unemployed for a much longer period of time. As a result, the unemployment rate for the older workers is often double that of the national rate (for example, in Germany and the United Kingdom). The French report notes that in 1979, unemployed males ages 15–24 were unemployed on an average of 7.1 weeks. Their elders, above age 50, were in this situation for 16.9 weeks. The comparable figures for women were 9.3 and 17.4 weeks (Paillat and Chesnais, 1980). Some elderly become discouraged and retire early, but some of them must be eager to return to the ranks of the active.

Considerable thought, often embodied in legislative initiatives, has been given in the United States (but less so in Europe) to involuntary methods of delaying the actual retirement of the aged—through raising the normal pensionable retirement age to 68 or higher. Depending on the phasing-in period, such a move would indeed relieve the financial crisis of all government old-age pension systems, possibly even with a margin for liberalizing benefits or reducing contributions. With proper safeguards for the interests of the presently insured, the increased retirement age could be phased in so as to meet the crunch in the contributor/beneficiaries ratio in the coming century.

Although none of the five European reports indicates current support for an upward change in retirement age, it might become a serious option for the *future*—if the effects on social security finances of an aging population coinciding with an aging and shrinking labor force are more clearly discernible.

Given the current obstacles to the immediate adoption of an increased pensionable retirement age, this reluctance to change is quite an understandable reaction. Sweden has only recently lowered the retirement age from 67 to 65. A reversal so soon after the downward change would be politically unsupportable. Furthermore, in all five countries, the trend toward a general lower retirement age, outright or through the extension of early and flexible retirement options, still runs strong. Until it is reversed—through lowering the benefit level, through the effect of inflation on the early retiree's total income, or through unforeseeable changes in the political, economic, and labor-market climates—raising the retirement age will be held in abeyance.

Understandable as such an attitude in the five European countries may be, it is perhaps shortsighted. Retirement norms in social security laws affect present-day retirement planning of individuals. Only 20 years divide the government planning of social security financing, as well as that by the insured, from the time when raising the retirement age is contemplated in the United States. Signaling the intended change now not only allows the insured to adjust all other steps inherent to retirement at a later age, but enables the actuary to build this fact into forecasts of future social security pension expenditures and the appropriate revenues to cover them. In predominantly contributory systems, this process determines the size of contributions to be paid now. If actuaries cannot count on a higher retirement age, they will arrive at a higher contribution rate than that which would be necessary if workers remained employed for a longer period of time. This is an important issue in a period of declining earnings, certain to affect public support of the entire social security system. Other forms of financing require similar adjustments.

9
European Approaches
to the Aging Problem

Although experts in the five European countries recognize the problems of the weakening contributor/pensioner ratio, they display no sense of urgency or doubt about their ability to meet a financial social security crisis. Some of them take comfort in the assumption that the crisis will not be on them until the turn of the century, and that the next decade may offer some relief for benefit expenditures. Others believe that increasing revenues through raising contributions in the future would not meet substantial opposition, and that any tax revolt can be contained.

At the same time, it is clear that in the present state of the economy, and at present rates of unemployment with no assured relief in sight, the European public retirement income programs are not going to expand greatly. This holds true even for the United Kingdom, whose energy outlook because of North Sea oil, rich coal reserves, and a growing nuclear power base, is somewhat rosier. However, attention has shifted in that country to the needs of other segments of the population, such as the handicapped, youth, one-parent families, and other groups requiring transfer payments and public assistance. Consequently, further liberalization of retirement pay will face severe competition in that country.

Attempts to reduce government expenditures to curb inflation, the emergence in some countries of conservative thought on reducing the role of the government, and a cutback of the social security pension program in spite of its popularity may threaten many retirement systems.

These factors explain the heightened interest in private pensions in many countries (Chapter 7) as well as the encouragement of a greater degree of labor-force participation by the older workers, both of which could reduce benefit expenditures of the state system and increase revenues (Chapter 8). From the viewpoint of society, both remedies may turn out to be more costly, although these costs may be offset in the second approach by the value of the goods and services which older workers would produce. The value of the additional output must be weighed against (1) the cost involved in stimulating the older individuals to seek work and in providing employment opportunities for them, and (2) the effects of increased older worker employment on the opportunities for other competing age groups—in particular, women and new entrants into the labor force. However, not every type of older-worker employment competes with that of other parts of the labor force. Some work, for example, calls on the expertise of the elderly, which is not necessarily readily available elsewhere.

Keeping older workers in the production process or providing them with other jobs would likely be a precondition for raising the normal statutory pensionable age in Europe, where legislators are generally influenced by the widespread support for social insurance and the trend toward early retirement. Therefore, they have so far shunned easy political solutions. Seeking a later retirement age might fall into this category, since such provisions would affect their constituencies only 10 or 20 years later. Only if the public and the legislature perceive that the number of aged persons working beyond the current minimum retirement age limits is substantial and is increasing could raising the retirement age be widely accepted and enacted into law. Otherwise, this measure would probably be opposed by those who fear that the savings in public pension programs might be offset by an increased burden on unemployment-compensation schemes and old-age or unemployment assistance (means-tested) programs. The prospect would be grim indeed if large numbers of aged persons able and willing to work could not find employment and were deprived of their retirement pay for an even longer period of time. Such an outcome could also lead to undesirable social and political consequences.[1] The opposition will also point out that the beneficial effects on social security finances of a higher retirement age are likely to be somewhat limited. Society may still want to maintain the well-entrenched early retirement provisions for special groups: older workers in arduous, hazardous, and unhealthy occupations; the handicapped; persons unable to work; the long-term unemployed; long-service workers; and workers with serious health problems who are not entitled to disability pensions.

ENCOURAGING OLDER WORKERS AND PENSIONERS TO WORK

The five European countries reject the one way which may have the most immediate effect: economic pressure through permanent outright reduction of the old-age benefit or through reduced indexing. Reports from these countries, however, suggest a number of other ways by which the employment of older workers can be increased.

The most promising avenue to the employment of the elderly is to keep them in those jobs where their experience counts and exceeds any possible loss of speed, endurance, reflexes, physical strength, and flexibility. In such jobs, the effects of aging can be compensated by the worker's knowledge, which may not be easily transferable to other employers and occupations. If necessary, continued employment can be facilitated by transfers, paid educational leave, change in shifts, improved environment, rearrangement of working hours, job redesign, transition to part-time work, and similar measures, or updated through training. Continued employment of older workers may be more easily accomplished in Europe, which tends to maintain the work force in slack periods and mild recessions. If necessary, this is done by reducing work hours. Even in France, which represents an exception of the rule,[2] 14 percent of the male retirees are still working, mostly in part-time jobs, especially when they can take advantage of a lower-than-usual retirement age (as is the case for railroad workers and employees).

Where unions, work councils, and shop stewards are strong (United Kingdom, Germany, France, Scandinavia), the older worker is protected against age discrimination by seniority and other provisions. In some European countries, the older worker is also safeguarded by severance-pay provisions that require the employer to pay a lump sum to the worker who is laid off. This payment, which is graduated according to length of service, serves not only as a complement to retirement pay and as a form of unemployment compensation, but also as a barrier against premature job loss. Stepping up the penalty payments for higher ages increases job security for the aged.

The authors of the country reports are well aware that changes in the social security system itself could increase the desire of the older worker to delay actual retirement. Among the positive measures to delay retirement is a sharp and progressive increase of the pension increment for the insured workers who remain in the labor force beyond normal pensionable age and the reduction or elimination of contributions on earnings beyond that age. Although, as mentioned earlier, current increment rates have not been effective in this regard anywhere, the picture may change if the increment is increased and is staggered according to the number of years of qualifying work. This action would also make the continued employment option under flexible retirement provisions more attractive. In view of the relatively small numbers of claimants now involved, it should not represent a heavy burden on the social security system. If, however, the increment were substantial and/or if sizable numbers of persons remained employed, the cost could be considerable.

Some European pension systems, like that in the United States, levy the payroll tax on the earnings of persons past the pensionable age, coupled with further increase of the benefit. In some cases (for example, France), the benefit is not increased. Other countries cancel the tax after the insured has reached normal pensionable age. Full or partial elimination of these contributions reduces the revenues of the social security system slightly, but it substantially increases the willingness of the employer to retain or hire older workers. It also increases interest on the part of the insured worker in remaining on the job. A similar result could be obtained by targeted income tax concessions.

Another measure would involve eliminating the earnings or retirement test that makes the receipt of the benefit contingent upon complete or partial withdrawal from the labor force. This exists in the United Kingdom[3] and the United States. In the Federal Republic of Germany, it exists for "flexible" retired workers between the ages of 63 and 65 and for qualifying female workers at 60. In some instances, the earnings test has proven to be one of the most effective barriers to substantial work beyond the retirement age, regardless of its technical construction (whether it still permits inconsequential hours of work and/or pay, or whether it reduces the pension gradually or eliminates it entirely). The unpopularity of the earnings test has forced some governments to liberalize provisions regarding severity and upper age limits. It may be abolished in the mid-1980s in the United Kingdom, and is scheduled to be reduced from age 72 to 70 in the United States in 1983.

One of the most important obstacles to the willingness of the aged to continue working beyond age 65 is the attractive pensions available upon early retirement. Reversing this trend through appropriate measures, such as drastically reducing the early retirement benefit, would have to precede the introduction of a higher pensionable retirement age. By itself, the reversal measure could more than offset the cost of higher retirement incentives and the elimination of earnings tests, as well as the loss of contributions levied upon the earnings of the workers 65 and older.

JOBS FOR AGED WORKERS

The more difficult task lies in finding new jobs for aged workers in the same line of work. Unless the new job is nearly identical to the old one, past experience may not be relevant.

Manpower measures, ranging from job sharing, mobility assistance, training and retraining facilities, employment quotas, sheltered jobs, and workshops, to subsidizations of the wage costs of businesses and public employment, could facilitate the older worker's labor-force reentry. France, for example, has established incentive bonuses for employers who recruit older staff in six regions facing economic difficulties (OECD, 1980). However, such measures may be opposed by organizations of the elderly, the unions, and employers as a type of preferment which invites opposition.

PART-TIME WORK

Opposition to measures mandated by law which give the elderly a preferential position in the labor market explains the frequent emphasis in the five
European reports on part-time work as a way for the elderly to work without
competing with other age and sex groups. The five European seminar reports
reflect a difference of opinion among policymakers, employers, and union
representatives as to whether there are sufficient new part-time jobs available
for the aged. The French appear more optimistic: between 1973 and 1979,
the percentage of 60- to 75-year-old males who were working part time
increased from 7.3 to 16.3; among females, the increase was from 23.1 to 31.1
percent. The United Kingdom paper is also guardedly optimistic on this
score for the period 1990–2000, although not necessarily for the present. The
three other countries find it more difficult to locate part-time vacancies for
the aged. In some countries, the upper limits of part-time jobs seems to have
been reached: 25 percent of the Swedish, and between 15 and 20 percent of
the Danish and United Kingdom, labor forces are employed part-time. In
the Swedish case, part-time work is favored not only by the partial pension,
but also by the impact of high marginal income tax rates and employer
preference based upon the lower absenteeism and higher productivity of
part-time workers. However, 9 out of 10 part-time workers are younger
women, leaving only a small residue of jobs for the older workers ("World
Leaders in Part-time Employment," 1980). To create new part-time jobs
would apparently require heavy subsidies, proportional in magnitude to the
cost of creating full-time public employment.[4]

In addition, to make part-time work more acceptable, steps would have to
be taken to protect the part-time worker from being the first to be laid off, to
enable him or her to participate in the firm's and the government's pension
program, to give part-time workers equivalent rights to those enjoyed by
full-time workers, and to prevent part-time work from feeding hidden unemployment. Intervention in the labor market in favor of workers 65 and
over is possible, but it is costly and may conflict with labor-market policies
directed toward assisting other preferred categories such as the young, the
unemployed, and women. Europe shares with the United States and other
countries the task of balancing and compromising conflicting social policies.
Each one, standing by itself and supported by public opinion and interest
groups, is valid, but it must compete with all others for budgetary consideration in an austere environment.

Some of the European countries seek compromise in staggered employment of the age groups 60 and over, gradually reducing the working hours
from full to partial employment. This prepares the worker for the reduction
of cash income that full retirement entails. It meets the psychological needs
of the worker for a gradual separation from routine, co-workers, status, and

working life (retirement shock). It also protects the interests of the employers. The interest in gradual retirement has kindled the interest in Sweden's
partial pension program, some aspects of which could be adapted to the
institutional needs of other countries.

SUMMARY

Two conclusions evolve from this discussion. First, the introduction of a
higher normal pensionable age requires a change in attitudes of older workers and their employers, as well as in society's views, as to when a person can
reasonably be expected to withdraw from the labor force. Since this date
may differ from one individual to another, the concept of a flexible retirement age within narrow limits (for instance, between the ages of 64 and 68 or
70) is nearly universally accepted in Denmark, France, Sweden, the United
Kingdom, and West Germany. Second, the voluntary employment of older
workers is considered desirable, but is hinged to the concept of gradual
retirement, preferably linked to a method of compensating the worker for
wage loss through some form of partial pension such as the Swedish one.
These two objectives could be attained through incentives to work at least
until, and preferably beyond, normal pensionable age.

The implementation of such a policy depends upon the future development of the quantitative and qualitative demand for the supply of labor. The
best chances for the employment of the elderly rest upon the existence of a
tight labor market, namely, labor shortages, as well as in continued employment in the jobs and occupations in which older workers gained their
experience, and on the emergence of vacancies that the aged are prepared
to fill.

10
Attitudes and Policy Responses

Although inflation threatens European workers and pensioners almost as much as—and in some countries, even more than—their American counterparts, our European co-researchers report no evidence that this factor by itself has yet induced workers to postpone retirement or encouraged pensioners to return to active work.

Of the two ways of prolonging work life—the compulsory approach through raising the retirement age (with exceptions for arduous and hazardous work, prolonged unemployment, ill health, and long-term service), or the voluntary method by making continued work more attractive—the consensus of public opinion in the five countries seems to favor the latter. However, one of the observers at the Danish seminar on retirement policy (Paul Milhøj) considers raising the retirement age together with incentives as the best way to limit the dependency burden upon the insured. The majority of opinions expressed in the seminars favor the voluntary way.

GOVERNMENT, EMPLOYER, AND UNION VIEWS

The German Ministry of Labor and Social Order opposes a higher retirement age, at least for the foreseeable future. It sees no need to reduce the standard of living of pensioners, but allows for a slowdown in the future benefit growth. It doubts that an increase in the number of old labor-force participants will ensure economic growth. For such growth, the ministry looks toward increased labor-force participation by women and foreign workers. On the other hand, it supports the idea of continued work of older workers by (a) more flexible retirement provisions and (b) the encouragement of gradual (step-by-step) reduction of working hours, which, in effect, could lead to deferred retirement on the basis of part-time work and partial pensions.

Although the representatives of the employers in the seminars can be presumed to hold a more positive view of a higher pensionable retirement age,[1] only the Swedish employers advocated it. They felt that an economy which was no longer growing demanded sacrifices from *all* parts of the population. Thus, the growing number of pensioners would have to expect lower and later pensions. Another Swedish group would consider raising the pensionable age only if all efforts to find jobs for the pensioners failed (Berglind and Bergroth, 1980). Employer attitudes are further analyzed below.

As would be expected, raising the retirement age was not welcomed by the unions. To them, a low retirement age represented a right, but not an obligation, for their members to retire. Nor were unions in the forefront of forces that sought to encourage the continued employment of working pensioners; they seemed more interested in assuring their members of the right to retire early with as large a pension as possible. To ensure future growth of the union, they may, so the French state, share in a de facto consensus with the employers which favors the younger workers. A more detailed analysis of the union interests is provided later in this chapter.

The Economic Climate

These reactions by government, employers, workers, and their unions must be understood in light of the economic situation in which they were formulated, the uncertainty of future changes of its parameters, and institutional restraints. Consideration must also be given to the prevailing trend toward earlier retirement, which was clearly identified as one of the major obstacles to a consideration of raising the retirement age and of encouraging the employment of older workers and pensioners.

THE GOVERNMENT DECISION

With the possible exception of Sweden, the countries face severe and non-abating unemployment: early retirement is supposed to open the career ladder to the young unemployed, who, if unaided, represent a potential threat to political stability. To provide one million jobs for the young, Giscard d'Estaing, in his quest for reelection in 1981, proposed to lower the age of early retirement to 58, to release workers over age 60, and to finance the repatriation of non-European immigrants. Job training for the young would also be expanded (*The Economist*, April 4, 1981, pp. 39–40). As employer representative Pointu emphasized at the French seminar on retirement-age policy, governments are, by nature, more inclined to act on short-run problems, to which they pay more attention (Paillat and Chesnais, 1980). Youth unemployment of the current magnitude is so considered. As a Danish Social Democratic Party representative allowed at the Danish seminar, the focus of social policy has shifted to children and the young (Friis and Hansen, 1980). The same is true for France (Pierre Laroque at the French seminar, in Paillat and Chesnais, 1980).

As long as high youth and other unemployment is perceived to be a short-term phenomenon, governments are not going to agree to permanent changes in retirement age. They are not going to lower it, as demanded by most unions (as in Denmark and Germany). Nor are they likely to raise it as long as they still cling to the hope that the retirement of older workers may open up job opportunities for young and other unemployed people. This sentiment is also reflected in the views of some employers.

The government, Patrick Moynihan once said, will act only if it can count the reasons for, and the effects of, a measure. This is difficult in a situation where the numbers of aged can be assessed for the period 1980–2030, but where the size or the age distribution of the total population, and the size and composition of the labor force so far ahead, cannot be assessed with any degree of certainty.[2]

Even if the ratio of the number of contributors to the number of pensioners could be assessed, the dependency burden also would have to take account of the respective size of the pension load and of earnings in order to arrive at a conclusion of the economic dependency rate; neither can be foreseen in the long-run. Were pensions to stay at their present level, for instance, while real earnings improved in the long-run at the same rate they did between 1948 and 1973 (when they increased by nearly 50 percent), even a much smaller but more productive labor force would be able to finance pension expenditures 25 years later. The conflict between the generations would be avoided. The present recession in the five European countries does not make such an outcome plausible, nor does it offer the government (and private pension funds) sufficient reliable evidence upon which permanent changes in the pension laws can be based.

Long-term social legislation which affects nearly the entire population, and which has nationwide political mass support, cannot—short of an imminent crisis, war, or collapse of the economy—be radically changed very easily. Changing the pensionable age, particularly in an upward direction, could be considered such a change. Whether the effects of the rising number of pensioners and a decreasing number of contributors will be perceived as an imminent danger to the pension load and the economy in Europe is not yet certain. In some countries, the effects of an aging population and labor force will become visible earlier than in others. In others, perceptions may be delayed until the next century. In all cases, however, public awareness of the problem has increased and will increase further in the future.

Instead of attacking the problem head-on in the social security arena, the government may prefer to achieve the same result of improving the financial status of the pension program indirectly by encouraging the employment of the older workers. This might be done through appropriate labor codes, manpower and tax measures, and marginal changes in the social security laws which are unlikely to meet much opposition.

THE EMPLOYERS' CONCERNS

Employers, although much concerned with the threat of increased social security contributions and, hence, not averse to raising the minimum pensionable age limit, could—if it were a closed economy—shift the increased cost-burden forward to consumers and taxpayers, or backward to labor. The former type of relief is not available in the competitive international market upon which the five European nations depend to a much greater extent than does the United States, with its greater reliance upon the domestic market. European business and economy depend much more upon exports for economic growth. As already intimated, success in this respect is sought primarily in high-technology industries, while the world market in traditional export products will be lost to the emerging developing countries (Eichner and Grossjohann, 1980). To man these industries, the employer representatives appear to prefer younger, better-educated, and better-trained workers. As a result, some employers favor early retirement schemes that permit changes in production techniques and the hiring of less costly younger workers. Early retirement turns into a management tool for the reduction of unit cost (CGT in France). A recent study of measures for sharing employment in the United Kingdom found that employers favored early retirement because they saw it as a cheap way to dispose the surplus work force. Early retirees are often not replaced when production techniques change, but, Fogarty points out, "this goes with reduction of the workforce rather than with any special effort to dispose of the elderly and unadaptable."[3] Other employers oppose premature retirement, not only because it increases pension expenditures, but because it leaves vacancies which are hard to fill, since there are no suitable young and unemployed to replace the retirees, and because general and total early retirement is not favorably received by the active labor force which—as taxpayers—must in large part support the pensioned population (Danish retirement-age policy seminar, Friis and Hansen, 1980).

THE BASIC UNION POSITION

The primary role of the unions is to defend the interests of their members and to maintain and strengthen the union's capability to do so in the future through increasing membership. As a rule, the unions concentrate their attention on current, short-run problems such as unemployment and inflation. Unions appear as the strongest supporters of early retirement, lower minimum pensionable-age limits, and higher benefits, as opponents to raising the retirement age limits, and as lukewarm supporters of continued labor-force participation of older workers (often a minority of members) and working pensioners. Future union strength rests on the ability to attract young members and to maintain the support of the majority of the current membership. For the older members, unions lay more stress upon their right to rest than upon their right to work. They see part-time work of the older manual workers as a threat to the union wage and labor standards.

If workers aim to reduce their work time (and work life) without loss of earnings, unions will support these demands and argue for overtime, higher benefits, and full retirement benefits at an earlier age (CGT in France, TUC in the United Kingdom, and DGB in Germany).[4] The unions justify this policy with reference to the rise in physical handicaps, premature disability, the boring character of manual work, and the (uncritical) view that pensioning-off older workers will cure unemployment.

Part-time work is also viewed as a threat to full-time employment. With a few exceptions (such as retail trade), it is often conceived as a downgrading of jobs that once were full time and as undermining labor standards and depressing wage levels, unless such outcome is prevented by law and collective agreement. Swedish part-time workers receive full medical benefits and full credit toward retirement. They must be allowed to remain in their part-time positions until age 70 ("Innovations in Working Patterns," 1981).

FLEXIBLE AND PART-TIME RETIREMENT

Attitudes toward the employment of older and retired workers differ within governments and among employers and union groups. There is, however, general support for workers' freedom to choose, within a relatively wide margin, the age when they will retire. This support also extends to their freedom of reducing the working hours in the years preceding retirement (part-time work). The "right to work" limited to age 70 is acknowledged, but there is some difference of opinion as to how this "right" can be enforced when seeking new employment. Bernard Bechet, deputy director of ARRCO in France, has raised a very poignant question: "Are there no other means for fulfillment than work?" And Andre Kirchberger of the OECD sees a contradiction in a policy which excludes active workers at earlier and earlier ages while there are efforts to insert the elderly into the ranks of the employed (Paillat and Chesnais, 1980).

OBSTACLES TO THE EMPLOYMENT OF THE AGED

Opposition to the reintegration of worker-pensioners sees obstacles on both the demand side and the supply side. The shortage of part-time work has already been discussed. On the demand side, some of the European co-researchers assert that the ability of the older worker to keep on working is seriously weakened in times of stagnating or decreasing real income. Looking to the supply side, the insured, fearful of inflation, may not be eager to postpone to an uncertain future some of the rewards (pensions) they might get today. A few Swedish voices doubt the ability of older workers to acquire the necessary qualifications, which they may not possess because of low or obsolete education. They also fear that workers may hesitate to undergo much training, if such an effort deprives them of means-tested or income-tested welfare benefits (like a housing allowance).

Representatives of the aged maintain the right of the worker to choose between work and retirement. They consider *active* retirement a right, independent of the need to work (United Kingdom). The Danish counterpart conditions this right on the availability of jobs. The cost-effectiveness of training older workers with limited work-life expectations has also been questioned.

SUMMARY

All in all, European views appear to arrive at a preference for "retraite à la carte," (Paul Paillat in Paillat and Chesnais, 1980)—the freedom of the workers to select, within certain age limits, the time and modus of retirement (full-stop or staggered reduction of working hours; part-time work). This posture appears to combine some features of Germany's flexible retirement and Sweden's partial pension plan. The future will tell whether the combination of these two concepts, together with improved financial incentives for continued work beyond pensionable retirement age, is able to reverse the trend toward early retirement and to encourage the insured to delay retirement, with beneficial results for the pension system and the economy.

11

Facing the Aging Problem in the United States[1]

Perhaps nowhere have the economic consequences of an aging population been more widely debated than in the United States. Certainly, of the six countries examined in this study, it is the only one where a higher retirement age seems a distinct possibility.

As is the case in Europe, the most pronounced impact of past demographic trends in the United States will not be felt until after the turn of the century, when the large postwar baby boom cohorts begin to reach what is now normal retirement age. Yet the social security system—the mainstay of economic support in old age—is in trouble. Some would call it a crisis. Sustained rates of high inflation, high unemployment, mortality improvements at the upper ages,[2] and early retirement trends have severely threatened the solvency of the Old Age and Survivors Insurance (OASI) trust fund.

Recognition of the problem has, in many instances, been long in coming. In late 1979, the Advisory Council on Social Security concluded that "all current and future social security beneficiaries can count on receiving the benefits to which they are entitled." The council further maintained that "the methodology now used to make financial projections is sound and the assumptions are reasonable." Just a few months later, however, another group contended the opposite, namely that the social security system was not soundly financed and that its ability to pay future benefits would be jeopardized unless sound financing was introduced to the system. This alarmist note now pervades public discussion about social security.

Warnings of a potential social security crisis have been sounded for some years; however, politicians have been, and remain, extremely reluctant to tamper with so venerable an institution, if that means reducing current benefits or reneging on commitments to future retirees. Since the program was established in 1935, almost all of the modifications have been improvements.

SUPPORT FOR THE AGED

In absolute terms, the costs of supporting a retired population are enormous. Programs providing the elderly with retirement income, health care, and

96

various social services have risen from 13 percent of the federal budget in 1960 to nearly 25 percent in 1981. As a percentage of GNP, public and private retirement-income programs have also increased. OASI benefits alone, for example, amounted to 0.3 percent of GNP in 1950; by 1978, they amounted to 3.8 percent.

Those statistics reflect a real rise in social spending for the elderly. Per capita expenditures for people over 65 have risen faster than the growth in productivity and inflation, mostly as a result of new programs and higher benefits. As happened in Europe, the infusion of federal dollars into programs for the elderly occurred against a backdrop of economic prosperity. High rates of growth enabled the federal government to expend social initiatives for the elderly without substantially reducing allocations to other segments of the economy. Expectations of a strong federal role in the maintenance of the aged's welfare and standard of living were fueled by the climate of accelerated productivity and high social spending (Samuelson, 1980). Those expectations may no longer be realistic in light of recent economic developments.

Declining rates of economic growth, soaring costs of energy and raw materials, and continued inflationary pressures have darkened prospects for an ever-increasing rate of economic growth and quantity of national wealth. Demographic trends will push even higher the retired aged population's need for a greater share of the economic pie. Some experts doubt that the economy will produce enough income to satisfy the additional demand.

The central issue is where the money for future benefits will come from. To the extent that the taxpayer (1) is able to maintain, or preferably improve, his or her standard of living and (2) can be assured of a reasonable return on his or her social security and private pension investment in the future, there would be little reason to anticipate any substantial shift in attitudes toward social security or support for the elderly. High rates of inflation, however, make it increasingly difficult for the average worker to maintain, let alone improve, that standard of living. At the same time, recipients of social security (and other public pensions) are guaranteed some inflation protection in the form of automatic cost-of-living increases that are not accorded all active workers.

SUPPORT FOR SOCIAL SECURITY

Probably no social program in the United States has benefited from support as widespread as that accorded social security. As of 1979, over 90 percent of all workers in the United States were covered under social security. The fundamental contribution that this program has made to the present generation of retirees obviously accounts for its popularity among that group. The expectation that they will eventually benefit from the system as well provides an incentive to current workers to continue to support the system by paying higher social security taxes when necessary.

Approximately 20 million older Americans receive retired-worker benefits from social security, which is by far the most important source of financial support in old age. Women, in particular, depend heavily on social security benefits either earned by them or, more commonly, by a spouse. Social security is the only source of income for 6 out of 10 older single, widowed, or divorced women.

About 28 percent of all retired married couples and about 14 percent of all single individuals receive private pension benefits. In the future, a greater percentage of older Americans can expect to see their social security benefits supplemented by income from another pension,[3] although expanded private coverage seems to be tapering off (President's Commission Pension Policy, 1981). Some 60 percent of the current generation of workers still anticipate that social security will constitute their primary source of income in retirement (President's Commission on Pension Policy, 1980b; National Commission on Social Security, 1981). Understandably, workers and the self-employed have a strong vested interest in social security, and support for the program runs high.

In fact, this support runs to higher contributions over reducing retirement benefits. When given the choice (hypothetically, at least), the American public was three times as likely to oppose lowering social security taxes as they were to oppose a reduction in retirement benefits. When a variation of the question was asked, these same respondents were even more emphatic: 63 percent opted for higher payroll taxes and 15 percent for lower benefits (Hart, 1980).

Despite the widespread support for social security, the public is by no means confident that the system will be able to pay their benefits when they retire. A 1978 survey, for example, found that 6 out of every 10 adults had doubts about the future of social security—up from 4 out of 10 just three years previously (American Council of Life Insurance, 1978). About two-fifths of the respondents in a 1979 Harris survey had "hardly any confidence that [social security] would be able to pay their benefits when they retire." Just as many questioned the willingness of future generations to pay the higher taxes that will be necessary to support retirees over the next several decades. Doubts like these could ultimately lead to resentment about higher contributions to support benefit increases for the already retired.

For a time after social security taxes were raised in 1978, it appeared as if a taxpayer's revolt might be in the offing, although contribution rates in the United States are typically lower than those prevailing in most European countries. Apparently, some members of Congress were besieged with enough constituent complaints to recommend a tax rollback, which, however, never materialized as resentment abated shortly thereafter. Little opposition was expressed when the contribution rate was increased again the following year.

Still, there may be limits to what workers are willing to "sacrifice" for the retired population, especially in view of the fact that in recent years, wages have not risen as fast as prices. Social security benefits, though typically low to begin with, are currently automatically adjusted to the consumer price index. The equity of guaranteeing such protection to retirees, when large numbers of workers do not receive comparable protection, has been called into question. In fact, automatic benefit indexing is under increasing attack.

Such concerns underlie some of the proposals, discussed subsequently, to shore up the social security system. Nevertheless, it is important to emphasize that in the United States, as in the European countries that we examined, no real conflict among the generations currently exists. So far, the elderly retain their status as a favored group among the public. An especially favorable orientation has been noted by the American Council of Life Insurance: in its 1979 survey of the general public, almost three-fourths of the respondents contended that government spending for the elderly should be increased, while only 22 percent felt this way about increased spending for minorities.

RETIREMENT AGE

Retirement age is an important consideration in the career plans of the average worker. As one member of the House Subcommittee on Social Security has noted, "if there is anything fixed dead center in the consciousness of our fellow countrymen, it is that 65 is the retirement age" (Jacobs, 1979, p. 72).

To be more precise, what is "fixed" in the consciousness is likely the expectation of pre-65 retirement. The introduction of early retirement provisions in social security and other pension systems has resulted in an increase in early (before age 65) withdrawal from the labor force, so actual retirement generally occurs well before 65. Almost 7 out of 10 older workers now opt for early—and permanently reduced—social security benefits. Sixty-two is the earliest and most common retirement age. Some of these early retirees leave voluntarily, but many others retire early because of health reasons, unemployment, or employer persuasion.

Less than 13 percent of the 65-plus population remain in the labor force, down from 27 percent in 1950, a decline that is predominantly accounted for by the sharply reduced participation rates of older males—almost 46 percent in 1950 versus 18.5 percent in 1981. To date, relatively few older persons (65-plus) have taken advantage of the 1978 amendments to the Age Discrimination in Employment Act which raised the mandatory retirement age to 70 in the private sector and eliminated it entirely in most branches of the federal

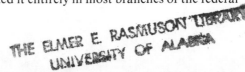

government. The reason for this seems clear: with a majority of workers opting for early (pre-65) retirement, interest in post-65 employment was a relatively rare occurrence before the amendments. Nor did employers put obstacles in the path of early retirees.

Given these work and retirement trends, it is highly doubtful that a legislated increase in retirement age would be received with equanimity. The 1979 national survey of the American Council of Life Insurance found that public sentiment against raising retirement age did indeed run strong: three-fourths of the respondents opposed any such change, even if introduced gradually over the next 25 years or so.

When the choice is between higher social security payroll contributions or an increase in retirement age some 20 years hence, the higher contribution burden still wins out. According to another national survey (Hart, 1980), just over half oppose a measure to raise retirement age, while only somewhat more than one-third are in favor.

PROPOSALS TO RAISE RETIREMENT AGE

Circumstances have brought the feasibility of current retirement age policies into question. A shrinking labor force, a growing aged dependent population, the economics of supporting the aged, and the biomedical dimension of increased life expectancy have placed severe pressures on social security. Simply stated, the program cannot meet future obligations without additional revenue.

Suggestions to raise retirement age have been heard with increasing frequency in recent years. Proponents of these changes argue that a later retirement age would effectively cut the costs of retirement programs. The impetus for a reevaluation of retirement policy has come largely—though not completely—from the rising costs of supporting an aged dependent population. First, the length of time over which benefits are paid to the individual retiree would be reduced. Second, the total number of beneficiaries at a given time would also be smaller. Third, the solvency of social security and other pension plans would be improved by an increase in the number of taxpaying contributors. Finally, overall economic output might rise as a result of higher labor-force participation, although opponents of a later retirement age maintain that an increase in older—and, they believe, less productive—workers would not have this desirable outcome.

Some observers believe that adjusting retirement-age policy is not a politically practical response to the problem of a rapidly aging society. It has been argued (for example, by Schulz, 1980a) that raising the retirement age for social security, even if made effective at some future date, would shake public confidence in the system and rupture the social contract on which social security has been based. In the midst of a headline-grabbing debate over the future solvency of social security, changes in a fundamental aspect of the system—like retirement age—could deepen any fears among workers that their benefits will not be there when they need them, and hence could precipitate the intergenerational conflict. Nevertheless, the possibility of a later retirement age has been raised by congressional committees, the research community, and the national study groups charged with exploring retirement policies.

Raising the social security retirement age is not a totally new idea. For instance, the 1975 Social Security Advisory Council,[4] as part of its analysis of social security financing, suggested that a later retirement age "might merit consideration in the next century." The advisory council went on to note that the demographics of an aging population could place an excessive burden of social security taxes on the labor force if retirement-age provisions were not changed in the future.

The 1979 advisory council, while clearly divided on many aspects of retirement-age policy, recommended that serious consideration be given to gradually raising the retirement age beginning around the turn of the century. In addition, the majority voiced objection to early retirement provisions. Representatives of organized labor, however, resoundingly denounced the proposal to raise the retirement age, and suggested further liberalization of early retirement provisions.

While there was no consensus on retirement-age policy, the tenor of the advisory council's discussion of the issues indicates that retirement age will receive more attention in the future. First, an attempt was made to assuage labor's objections to raises in the retirement age by also urging consideration of special unemployment insurance for older workers. The unemployment insurance suggested was to be "sufficient to make it unnecessary for older workers to claim early retirement benefits" and "paid as long as the worker was ready and able to work until the worker reached age 65" (Advisory Council on Social Security, 1979, p. 180). Current administration efforts to limit federal financial aid for unemployment insurance cast some doubt on this solution. Even reduced unemployment benefits are, as a rule, higher than pensions.

Of all the study groups that have investigated retirement policy, few have had as broad an agenda as the President's Commission on Pension Policy. Established by executive order and instructed to conduct a comprehensive overview of national retirement policy, the commission demonstrated an inclination to approach the analysis of retirement policy from the perspective of national social and economic policies.

In researching retirement age over almost two years of public meetings, the commission explored the effect of retirement trends on a variety of retirement systems and made several suggestions with regard to raising retirement age. First, it made note of the demographic change toward an older population and a smaller labor force. Second, it documented the early retirement trend among those employees receiving public or private pensions, noting that reevaluation of retirement ages in various pension plans would depend upon cost factors specific to the retirement system in question. Third, it addressed shortcomings in present unemployment-insurance and career-transition policies that produced higher rates of involuntary retirement by forcing workers to utilize disability or early retirement provisions. Fourth, it noted a lack of incentives to remain working at older ages, and suggested adopting measures such as the phasing out of the social security earnings test (contingent upon a recommendation that social security contributions and benefits receive the same tax treatment as other retirement programs) and the possible elimination of mandatory retirement.

Among the many recommendations of the President's Commission on Pension Policy was one to raise retirement age to 68 gradually over a 12-year period beginning in 1990. Early retirement would be raised in tandem to 65.

The commission had several justifications for its recommendations. First, life expectancy has increased substantially since 1935, and it is likely—the commission felt—that this trend will continue. Second, the commission observed that workers are healthier today and many jobs less strenuous than in the past. These two developments should make it easier for older workers to remain employed. In the event that health problems preclude employment, the commission recommended that more easily obtainable disability benefits be provided. Finally, in view of the severe strain on the financing of social security anticipated when the baby-boom generation retires, a three-year delay in retirement would, the commission felt, substantially alleviate the drain on the system.[5]

The National Commission on Social Security was a bipartisan, nine-member group established by Congress in December 1977 to conduct a comprehensive study of all aspects of social security and related programs and to develop a long-range blueprint for change that would create "a system that would best serve the Nation in the future" (National Commission on Social Security, 1981). In its final report of March 1981, this commission made a similar recommendation to raise retirement age and the age for Medicare eligibility to 68 in the twenty-first century, through legislation enacted now. The rationale for this proposal resembles, in part, that of the President's Commission on Pension Policy: increased life expectancy and a worsening ratio of workers to retirees. Moreover, this commission believed that older workers will be in greater demand in future years and that "given sufficient notice, coming generations of beneficiaries can adjust to a later retirement age just as earlier generations adjusted to 65." Such a change would generate savings estimated at 1.07 percent of payroll.

Unanimity with regard to the retirement-age proposal did not characterize the recommendation to raise retirement age. Three members of the commission dissented, arguing that the reasons for the proposal were not persuasive. In particular, they did not subscribe to a "gloom-and-doom" scenario that projects that the American economy in the future would not permit the continued payment of full benefits at age 65.

The dissenters also argued that there is little evidence to suggest that longer life is equivalent to longer years of good health. Increasing life expectancy has, they note, been accomplished by earlier retirement, which is not necessarily coincidental: a reduction in work stress may improve health status and—consequently—life expectancy. Because health problems cause so many older workers to retire, additional disability costs could increase, thus raising the question of the size of savings to the system.

As is often the case with commissions such as the two discussed above, all of the efforts of their members seem to have been for naught. President Reagan has decided that another working group (National Commission for Social Security Reform) should examine social security's funding problem and recommend solutions. Since its final report is not due until the end of 1982, members of Congress are spared the politically untenable burden of grappling with social security during an election year (1982). Their understandable reluctance to come to grips with the subject has been aided once again by the establishment of a commission that permits them to postpone implementing what could prove to be some extremely unpopular policies. Another delay, however, while perhaps good for the politicians, is not necessarily for the good of social security.

Although recommendations to raise retirement age have been voiced in many circles, almost every proponent has advocated a gradual phase-in so that workers would have adequate time to reevaluate their work and retirement plans. An immediate increase would, most experts agree, be unreasonably punitive. For similar reasons, the 1981 proposals of the Reagan administration to restore the integrity of the social security system through immediate lowering of early retirement benefits were widely received with shock and alarm, and were quickly retracted once the intensity of opposition became apparent.

The administration has made it "perfectly clear" that it has no intention of raising retirement age to 68. Rather it wishes to reinforce the notion of 65 as the normal—and appropriate—retirement age. As noted previously, a worker with sufficient years of covered employment is entitled at age 62 to early retirement benefits that amount to 80 percent of what he or she would have been entitled to at the full retirement age of 65. The proposed changes would have reduced the age-62 benefit to 55 percent of the full-benefit amount. An average wage earner entitled to a monthly benefit of $372.80 under present

Table 11.1. Social Security Benefits Comparison for 62-Year-Old Worker

Year and Earnings Category[1]	Under Law, 1981	Under Reagan Proposal, 1981	Percent Difference
1982			
Low	$247.60	$163.90	−34
Medium	372.80	246.80	−34
Maximum	469.60	310.50	−34
1987			
Low	384.40	225.20	−41
Medium	580.70	348.30	−40
Maximum	755.60	430.00	−43

[1] Low-, medium-, or maximum-wage earner.

law would have received instead $246.80—or one-third less (Table 11.1).[6] Moreover, the administration proposed introducing the reduction for all workers retiring on or after January 1, 1982—a proposal that represented a radical departure from other retirement-age proposals. This change would have been accompanied by another that reduced the income-replacement ratio of the average worker by 3 percentage points (from 41 to 38 percent) in the next five years, a modification designed to correct past overcompensation of retirement benefits that would further reduce anticipated benefits.[7] Extremely harsh early retirement penalties would, after a probable rush of retirements prior to enforcement, undoubtedly force many unwilling workers to postpone retirement, and eventually "reinforce the notion" of age 65 as the appropriate retirement age.

Severely penalizing early retirees and reducing replacement rates under social security were but two of the reform proposals of the Reagan administration. The enactment of *all* the proposals would, according to the administration, have resulted in a social security system that is actuarially sound over the short- and long-range. In addition, even under their "worst-case" economic assumptions, the social security tax increase in 1985 would have been lower than that now scheduled; a substantial *reduction* in taxes promised for 1990 (a tax rate of 6.45 percent for employers and employees, instead of the scheduled 7.65 percent). The concurrent reduction in the employers' share did not remain unnoticed.

Under most circumstances, workers can hardly be expected to decry a social security—or any other—tax decrease. Social security tax cuts, however, may well prove the exception. To date, the American public has voiced its opinion that higher social security taxes are preferable to lower social security benefits. There may indeed by a point at which the insured population would demand that the retired share some of the burden of declining growth rates. However, we have no idea just what that limit might be; questions about hypothetical tax rates are relatively meaningless. It is not until the worker observes his or her paycheck that the bite can really be felt. As things stand now, the administration's proposals appeared to fly in the face of public sentiment vis-à-vis social security taxes and retirement benefits. Legislators are not unmindful of this.

OTHER PUBLIC RETIREMENT PROGRAMS

Funds for other public retirement benefits have also been subject to public scrutiny. Because social security provides the bulk of retirement benefits, it is typically the focus of concern. However, public and private pension plans also cover a significant portion of workers and retirees, and these pension schemes also face problems similar to those of social security. Regardless of the method of financing, the same result can develop: competing claims over distribution of a nation's output between workers and pensioners. The aging of the labor force has brought many pension-plan members close to or into retirement. Early retirement options and other liberalization of eligibility criteria have added to the number of actual and potential beneficiaries. These pension systems have consequently begun to experience a drain on their financial resources.

The Congressional Budget Office (CBO) recently warned that unless changes were introduced, costs for federal retirement programs (for example, civil service and military) would more than double over the next five years as a consequence of inflation and the addition of almost one-half million more retirees by 1986. Annual expenditures could soar from almost $15 billion to $30 billion. Cost-of-living increases would account for nearly 70 percent of this increase (Causey, 1981).

Currently federal retirees typically fare substantially better than their counterparts under social security. A federal worker can retire as young as 55 with 30 years of service. If an agency is undergoing a reduction in force or reorganization, the Office of Personnel Management may, as it has in the past, permit immediate retirement to workers at age 50 with 20 years of service or at any age after 25 years. (Procedures for approving early-outs have been tightened in recent months.) Up to the present, such retirees have been able to enter the private sector and accumulate credits toward a social security or private pension, which substantially enhances their financial status when they retire "for good."

The true costs of federal pensions amount to some 30 percent of payroll (Causey, 1981). To reduce future growth, the Congressional Budget Office has recommended a sharp increase in employee contributions to the pension fund (employees now pay 7 percent) or a reduction in the size and frequency of future cost-of-living increases. Another CBO option involves a phase-in of reduction for pre-65 retirement: a 10 percent reduction at age 60 and a 25 percent reduction at 55. Such a move could prompt a higher retirement age on the part of some workers; however, the experience of social security—with a 20 percent reduction in benefits at age 62—would suggest that such a reduction might not have a significant effect upon actual retirement age.

In its final recommendation, however, the President's Commission on Pension Policy went a step further with regard to retirement age. The commission's final report states that "a retirement age policy that parallels that of social security is recommended for all federal retirees." The commission recommended phasing in a normal retirement age of 65 for all new retirees; this age would increase in tandem with the increases under social security.

Proposals designed to solve the problem of financing in retirement-income systems have generally involved explicit or implicit cuts in benefits to the already retired, and it is such proposals that mobilize lobbyists for the aged and others, such as organized labor, to action. So far, they have managed to prevent any substantial encroachment into retirement benefits. President Carter promised delegates to the 1981 White House Conference on Aging that budget cuts would not affect any programs for the elderly (*Washington Post*, 3/27/80), although it should be pointed out that only three days later, budget cuts did threaten to affect at least one such program in a major northeastern city (*Boston Herald*, 3/30/80).

It is not just organized interest groups which so far have been effective in minimizing budget cuts in programs for the elderly. Those most threatened by budget cuts (55–74 years old) themselves respond by voting proportionately more than younger taxpayers. The potential political consequences of this fact cannot be ignored, because politicians are also aware of the power of the "seniors' ballot" or at least *perceive* their voting as influential and partly determined by their age and/or retirement status. In Florida, where the 65-plus voters comprise 18 percent of all voters, the net result of their voting behavior is interpreted as becoming "more for the old, less for the young" (Gustaitis, 1980). With the reduction in economic growth, the current allocation of resources might further deplete resources for other age groups unless they fail to register their protest through voting. Unless the economic picture brightens substantially, this outcome might be inevitable.

SUMMARY

The administration has backed away from its earlier proposals to tamper drastically with social security. Public reaction to those (and other) proposals to tamper with the system has not gone unnoticed by other politicians, who are justifiably fearful of the consequences of supporting sizable social security benefit reductions; and a higher retirement age can be perceived as a benefit reduction. An election year is not an auspicious time to move in this direction.

Nonetheless, American workers should probably resign themselves to the fact that social security is no longer sacrosanct, especially in this budget-conscious era.[8] They might well adjust themselves to the eventuality of working beyond "normal" retirement age. An increase in retirement age probably will not occur without a fight, and it undoubtedly would be phased in over a period of time, but the tide in the United States seems clearly to be moving in the direction of redefining upward what is now perceived as normal retirement age.

12

Summary and Conclusions

OVERVIEW OF FINDINGS

The United States is not alone in facing the problems of an aging population and labor force. As our examination shows, Denmark, France, Sweden, West Germany, and the United Kingdom face, with minor differences, a similar demographic situation through the end of the century.

Despite an increase in the proportion of aged in every country except the United Kingdom through the year 2000, the overall dependency ratio is expected to decline over the next 20 years. This decline is largely the result of falling birthrates and a consequent drop in the youth dependency ratio. But, more significantly, relatively little deterioration of the aged dependency ratio is anticipated. Only in Germany is that burden expected to increase before the turn of the century, and even there it will be well below its 1977 level (table 3.1). Owing to previous fertility trends, the population of "working age" will continue to increase in each of these countries.

On the surface, therefore, the dependent support issue looks reasonably bearable over the short-term period of 20 years or so. These crude dependency ratios, however, obscure some very relevant facts. First, the older population itself is aging and, hence, more costly to maintain. This trend will continue until the large postwar cohorts reach their sixties around 2005 or 2010. Second, to an increasing extent, old-age dependency begins, not at 65, but, as a result of a variety of early retirement options and other factors, well before that age in many cases. Moreover, many of those persons of "working age" are not now—nor will they all become—contributors to retirement-income schemes.

The absolute cost of supporting these growing aged and retired populations has been convincingly documented by our European co-researchers, who do not deny that expenditures will continue to increase before the anticipated shrinking óf the working-age population after the turn of the century. Yet, they are not unanimous in their concern about the willingness or ability of the taxpayers in their respective countries to assume an additional support burden. In some countries, the unwritten social contract between the generations may be endangered.

None of the Europeans documented any appreciable interest in postretirement-age employment. Given the lack of interest in continued employment on the part of even the young old, coupled with high unemployment, it becomes understandable that public policy and concern will focus on other groups, such as the young and reentry women, who are able and eager to work. A projected expansion of the labor force (country reports and the ILO, 1977) suggests that, in terms of numbers alone, the ratio of *workers* to aged dependents will not deteriorate over the course of this century. A continuing trend toward earlier retirement, however, could upset this balance. Moreover, a larger share of the labor force will be comprised of women, whose salaries and hours worked will not necessarily serve as a sufficient offset to the loss of contributions from retiring male workers.

To some extent, the declining cohorts of young dependents may also serve as an offset to escalating costs of support for the aged in Europe and the United States. In terms of numbers alone, there is indeed such an offset through the turn of the century. The available data on costs of support, however, do not enable us to make any conclusions as to just how large any savings might be. Expenditures for the elderly are largely public ones, and, hence, readily identified and subject to scrutiny. The same is not true of the costs of raising children.

None of our European co-researchers places much stock in a biomedical development that might increase life expectancy substantially over the next several decades. Nor do official projections, on which policies are presumably based at least in part, assume much of an improvement in mortality rates or life expectancy. But even "modest" improvements in mortality, especially when concentrated at the upper ages, can have a noticeable impact on the number of persons living into very old age, as United States data have shown. It is here, of course, that health care and social service expenditures are particularly pronounced, as all of the European co-researchers have noted.

Berglind and Bergroth suggest that in view of the fact that life expectancy in Sweden is among the highest in the world, the likelihood of raising it further is probably not very great. However, directing attention to preventive health and medical care might have a positive effect on future health and service costs. In other words, the problems associated with an aging older population might, at some point, be offset by an improved health status within that older population.

In the event that the demand for labor exceeds the supply, Europe might turn again to immigrant labor before it undertakes to replenish its supply from the reservoir of aging and retired workers. Paillat and Chesnais even suggest that help for some European countries facing potentially chronic manpower shortages (for example, West Germany, Belgium, and Switzerland) might come from the excess French labor supply, until France's own labor shortage materializes after the turn of the century. An excess of labor that could supplement other shortages in other nations is hardly conducive to raising retirement age in a particular country.

Fogarty (United Kingdom) warns of an encroaching cold climate as far as expanded support for the elderly is concerned, in large part because of pressing demands from other underserviced segments of the population (such as youth and the handicapped). Paillat and Chesnais also warn that a backlash may develop in France if aged support costs continue to soar, and a similar possibility is mentioned by Eichner and Grossjohann for Germany. In neither case, however, is there documentation that such a development is imminent.

Friis and Hansen in Denmark and Berglind and Bergroth in Sweden take quite an opposite stand. In Denmark, "there is every reason to believe that almost any reduction in the expenses for the elderly will meet with strong resistance both among the younger and older people" (Friis and Hansen, 1980, p. 108). As Berglind and Bergroth report, official policy expressed by politicians maintains that the solidarity with old-age pensioners in Sweden "may be assumed to be very strong indeed," and that "the active part of the population can make rather great sacrifices to keep the promises, at least to the old age pensioners" (Berglind and Bergroth, 1980, p. 43). Berglind (1978) has warned that even in Sweden, risks of negative attitudes toward the supported exist in a high-taxation society with a stagnated economy and growing transfer payments. Nonetheless, politicians in Sweden intend, Berglind and Bergroth write in their 1980 report, to keep their promises to pensioners.

Friis and Hansen cite statistics which would certainly appear to support their observations. A 1973 Danish survey found that 62 percent of the population felt that under no circumstances should there be retrenchments in the old-age pension; 38 percent felt this way about nursing homes. Several years later, well after the energy crunch had begun to make itself felt, support for these two elements in the public budget seemed to be stronger: 73 percent of the respondents to a Gallup Institute survey published in 1980 again contended that under no circumstances should the old-age pension be touched. Some 44 percent opposed nursing-home cuts under any circumstances (Friis and Hansen, 1980).

We are not aware of comparable data for the United States, although public opinion on benefits and programs for the elderly, measured in numerous studies, does reveal strong support for programs for the aged, most particularly social security. As a 1980 survey on social security demonstrates clearly, "there can be little question that Americans reject the idea of lowering [those] benefits below current levels" (Hart, 1980, p. 70), even if the only alternative is higher taxes.

What the authors of these reports on retirement-age policy have not told us (nor is it likely that anyone knows) is whether—and when—resentment against higher taxes might foster a specific resentment against benefits for a growing number of reasonably young retirees. Friis and Hansen point out, for example, that only 19 percent of the Danes responding to the previously mentioned Gallup survey opposed retrenchment in the severance-pay scheme under any circumstances. Might this be regarded as opposition to perceived preferential treatment of a select group (for example, aged 60–66) of unemployed workers?

Wander (1978) has noted, and it bears repeating, that Europe has, at least until now, managed to meet the demands of a growing aged population—a refutation of the alarmist note voiced by observers of the trend toward zero population growth. As seen in table 2.1, as early as 1960, all of the five European countries were as "old" as the United States is now. The proportion of U.S. population 65 and older (11 percent) had been achieved in France and the United Kingdom in 1950. Moreover, at least since 1950, the labor-force participation rate of the aged population in each of these countries has been below that of the older population in the United States.

Whether the European support of the aged has been adequate is, of course, quite another question. Paillat and Chesnais stressed the very low old-age benefits in France in the 1950s and 1960s. But, with the aging of the population and with expanding economies, these countries were typically able to provide more and better services to their elderly, to improve retirement benefit levels, and to expand opportunities for earlier and earlier retirement. Can this trend continue?

Perhaps one of the more significant observations in this manuscript is that Sweden has recently reduced the income-replacement rate under the very popular, in fact too popular, partial pension scheme. Countries considering a similar program or a modification of it would do well to turn to Sweden for an evaluation of the tremendous costs of this exemplary retirement program.

Despite the desire for early retirement, these countries can expect an increasing reservoir of persons in the upper ages who are able, and perhaps even willing, to work. These people will, by the turn of the century, be better equipped by education and experience to increase the sum and the quality of the national output.

The utilization of these resources faces a number of obstacles at the present time. Some are likely to be of a transitory nature, as, for example, unemployment. Others, such as societal approval of early retirement or informal age discrimination, are more deeply rooted attitudes.

The need to provide an increasing part of the population with the necessary income, coupled with concerns about the ability of public and private pension programs to provide adequately for retirees, has raised the question of the dependency burden in each of these countries. There is no doubt that a growing economy with growing employment can shoulder this obligation, but questions have been raised as to whether either or both are likely to continue to grow at a satisfactory rate. The capacity of the economies to support a growing nonworking elderly population in the future remains uncertain.

Unfortunately, the discussion of this fundamental question has been obscured by the financial problem of the government social security programs. One of the major lessons of this study is to divorce the long-term, basically unanswerable, support burden problem from that of the best way of assuring the countries of a solvent public pension program. Chapters 5 and 6 reviewed a number of ways by which the economy can achieve the latter, ranging from reducing benefits to increasing revenues and shifting the emphasis from the public to the private sector.

The implication of this finding is that raising the normal pensionable age by three or more years, a step currently rejected by the five European countries, may assist in restoring solvency to the social security system's financial position. It will not, however, fully offset the increase in the aged dependency burden on the economically active population. Nor does a higher retirement age automatically ensure that the "young aged" (65–70) will be able to retain or obtain a role in the active labor force, or that society will take advantage of the potential contribution of the aged to the production of goods and services.

It is primarily for the last stated reasons that the five European countries are groping for a way which would enable the young-old workers to participate in the production process, commensurate with their competence and interest. This they see in the promotion of partial employment, preferably with some income support to compensate for the income loss inherent in offering less working time. This approach—exemplified by the unique Swedish partial pension—responds to labor and industry preferences, as well as to socio-gerontological considerations which favor gradual retirement over abrupt cessation of economic activity.

Once the practice of part-time involvement of the elderly is sufficiently widespread and generally accepted, raising the normal pensionable retirement age may find general approval and will also substantially reduce the support burden.

These observations may find an application in the United States. To translate them into fact may require taking some of the steps outlined in Chapters 7, 8, and 9, together with changes in the social security and unemployment insurance laws and private pension arrangements. They should not be confounded with the necessary steps to put today's social security system on a sound financial basis.

In conclusion, Denmark, France, Sweden, West Germany, and the United Kingdom are faced with problems that, although sporadically recognized in the past, were submerged in the period of postwar economic tranquility that fostered, among other things, the expansion of early retirement programs and improved benefits and services to the elderly. A labor shortage, high economic growth, and modest inflation are being replaced, to a greater or lesser extent, by rising unemployment and inflation and a stagnating economy. In view of the extent and recency of these problems, is it any wonder that a later retirement-age policy has not been accorded much attention? Early retirement programs have come to be regarded as social achievements in most, if not all, of these countries, and every indicator points to a continuation of the trend toward early labor-force withdrawal. Although this development may reflect a short-sighted perspective on the part of policymakers in Europe, attempts to reverse this trend through involuntary measures would meet with strong resistance. It is by no means certain that the undocumented savings generated by a higher retirement age would, at this point, be worth the political struggle.

CONCLUSION

We hope that we have made it clear in preceding chapters that government, employer, and—to a lesser extent—labor attitudes about retirement and retirement age in the five European countries differ from those in the United States. Leaving aside the possibility that, in time, European attitudes will come closer to those in the United States, or vice versa, the question arises as to what accounts for the difference.

The similarities of the socioeconomic position that Europe and the United States will face early in the twenty-first century have been highlighted: a growing dependency burden resulting from decreasing fertility and an increasing proportion of pensioners, a possibly shrinking demand for manual and other nonmanual workers, a slowdown in economic growth, and so forth. In the presence of unemployment and inflation, the short-term outlook for balancing the books of social security carriers and private pension funds is almost identical.

Management's opposition to many demands of organized labor is probably harsher in Denmark, France, Sweden, the United Kingdom, and West Germany than it is in the United States. Nor can the political coloration of the party in power alone explain the difference in position regarding retirement age. It may provide an opportunity for early retirement; however, proposals for raising the retirement age in the United States have emerged under both parties.

The United States cannot hope to offer workers between the ages of 65 and 68 proportionally more jobs than the Europeans. Nor is the United States less generous than the five European countries in the desire to offer adequate retirement income to the aged. The opposite comes nearer the truth.

The difference seems to lie in the degree of commitment to the social-insurance concept. Social insurance, the mechanism that provides the retired with income "as a matter of right" rather than need, is only about half as old in the United States as it is in Europe.

The pragmatic spirit that permeates life in the United States questions all institutions, while tradition governs in Europe. This attitude can also be seen in different attitudes toward unions and collective bargaining. The five European countries did not follow the United States example of enacting a Taft-Hartley Act or right-to-work laws; there are no questions of the value of collective bargaining.

The tie between organized labor and social security appears to be stronger in Europe than in the United States. Again, historical development has to be considered. Retirement pensions and their improvements are considered one of the major gains of the European labor movement, even in those countries where they originated by government action. In contrast, U.S. labor leaders Samuel Gompers and William Green, fearful that the unions would lose the credit for achieving income protection for retired union members through the bargaining process, hesitated to support social insurance legislation. Obviously, this does not hold for the present attitude of the AFL-CIO, which is among the staunchest defenders of government income-maintenance provisions in the United States. The AFL-CIO acts as the principal spokesman for the interests of 36 million social security beneficiaries and 4.1 million supplemental-security-income beneficiaries.

U.S. management is more prone than its European counterpart to attack or whittle down the retirement pension or to increase retirement age. European employers are, moreover, less likely to dislodge labor's representation in the various administrative bodies built into their respective social security programs. Longer experience has demonstrated for the enterprises the limits of private pension coverage and has enhanced their interest in the stability of industrial and pension relations.

The European concern for stability in both directions is less well developed in the dynamic U.S. economy. Hence, questioning the cost, location (public and private), and performance of the current pension system can be understood as another expression of a young and vital country, which prefers vigorous action to long-term analysis and which is always willing to risk making mistakes in the certain expectation of being able to remedy them when necessary.

The differences between Europe and America, while clearly discernible and perhaps even measurable, may well narrow over time. The ways in which they narrow and, in fact, the differences themselves are worthwhile indicators for scholars, practitioners, and policymakers involved in retirement-age policy. It is for this reason that an international perspective toward policy in this field should not be overlooked by national planners on both sides of the Atlantic.

POSTSCRIPT

A dramatic and significant postscript can be added to this book. Throughout, we have voiced the opinion that—despite concern over growing demands on retirement-income, health, and other support systems for the elderly—a higher retirement age does not appear to be in the cards for the five European countries covered in our study. If anything, we speculated that any change would be in the direction of a lower retirement age. Indeed, this is what has happened in one of the countries since our manuscript was completed: France has lowered its normal retirement age substantially.

As of April 1983, long-service employees with 37.5 years under the general scheme will be eligible to retire at age 60 with a benefit of 50 percent of their average earnings in their ten highest years. This 50-percent replacement rate is the most a worker will be able to receive upon reaching the new retirement age: bonuses for delaying retirement will be eliminated. Other changes, including provisions for persons with fewer years of service, are designed to reinforce a worker's decision to retire at 60. Among these is a requirement that workers who wish to remain employed beyond age 60 leave their current jobs and find *new* employment, a not-so-easy task for older workers. Any incentive to hire an older worker is not likely to be enhanced by the requirement that the worker and the employer both contribute to the unemployment-compensation fund.

The new retirement-age policy in France reflects the government's commitment to solving the unemployment problem, particularly among youths. If older workers retire, it is reasoned, job opportunities for youths will be expanded; however, the extent to which this actually happens remains to be seen.

While the sharp reduction in retirement age may be politically popular in the immediate future, it may eventually prove to have been a short-sighted move for at least two reasons. First, France's seemingly favorable dependency burden may, as discussed in Chapters 2-4, be deceptive. The dependent population is aging, as is the older population itself; expenditures for the elderly have increased markedly in France and will continue to escalate. It is quite possible that the actual costs of lowering retirement age will far exceed the government's rather modest estimates. Second, if the public comes to perceive age 60 as the retirement age it can depend on, reversing the recent decision, should that ever become necessary, would be an extremely difficult and painful decision.

Appendix A:
Evaluating Retirement-Age
Policy—The Research Design

The form in which the study was carried out consisted of essentially three steps:

- Preparation of a working paper on each country by the collaborating researchers for use in a seminar discussion of the issues
- A seminar, attended by representatives of key types of policy-influencing organizations, such as labor and employment federations, government officials and experts, pension organizers, and policy researchers
- A report on the policy responses and issues discussed at the seminar

This format was followed in each of the five European countries. In the United States, where policymakers at all levels have been discussing retirement policy for some years and where an earlier study by the American Institutes for Research sponsored seminars on retirement-age policy, only the working paper was prepared.

Within the broad mandate to examine the extent to which demographic, socioeconomic, and biomedical factors might necessitate a reevaluation of retirement-age policy, the study collaborators were to examine, in their respective countries:

- Demographic trends
- Labor-force trends and projections, including the changing ratio of workers to nonworkers
- Productivity trends that may affect the country's ability to support a growing aged population
- The extent to which early retirement is being proposed as a solution to unemployment
- Potential offsetting factors, such as increased labor-force participation on the part of women, that may reduce the current support burden
- The short- and long-run implications of current demographic trends
- Public opinion regarding retirement and the retirement support issue
- Measures, if any, to retain older workers in the labor force

- The response of policymakers in, for example, business, government, labor, and pension systems to retirement-age policy

The findings described in this book represent the authors' compilation of the material provided by the collaborators—the working papers and the seminar reports. In these chapters we have attempted to point out the similarities and differences among the countries' policy responses to issues concerning retirement age, projected future direction of retirement-age policy, controllable and uncontrollable factors affecting policy, and short- and long-term implications of various policy trends.

Wherever possible, we have based our discussion on the data provided by the European co-researchers. This is particularly the case in the earlier chapters, where demographic and labor-force trends are reviewed. In most cases, the data presented by the co-researchers were the most recent. More important, however, is the fact that their official statistics are, presumably, used by decision makers in the five countries to formulate policies concerning, among other things, the support of the elderly. In using these data, however, a question of comparability arises. Estimates and projections, for example, are frequently provided for different age groups and time periods. Moreover, the various co-researchers emphasized different aspects of the aging population, so data are not always available for every relevant topic. In some cases, these omissions reflect the co-researchers' own interests and priorities; in other cases, it appears that national statistics were unavailable.

Occasionally, data from other sources are used to supplement information from the country reports. We have attempted to avoid this step as much as possible, however, since we found that supplemental data (such as population projections from the ILO) were frequently very different from those used by the co-researchers. Only time will tell which assumptions and projections were more valid. We can simply assume that, for our purpose, the co-researchers' data are the most relevant, since they are generally official national statistics. We wish to point out, however, that the country reports were completed in 1980. Although we have updated some of the policy developments (for example, with respect to Sweden's partial pension and U.S. social security proposals), it is seldom possible in a policy paper to be completely up to date. The co-researchers are:

Denmark   Henning Friis
                 Per Vejrup Hansen
                 Socialforskningsinstituttet
                 (The Danish National Institute of Social Research)
                 28 Borgergade
                 DK-1300 Copenhagen

France	Paul Paillat
	Jean-Claude Chesnais,
	Institut National d'Études Démographiques
	(National Institute for Demographic Studies)
	27, Rue du Commandeur
	75675 Paris
Sweden	Hans E. Berglind
	University of Stockholm
	School of Social Work
	S-10691 Stockholm
	Alf Bergroth
	University of Östersund
	Box 373
	831-25 Östersund
United Kingdom	Michael P. Fogarty
	Policy Studies Institute
	1/2 Castle Lane
	SW1E 6DR London
West Germany	Harald Eichner
	Klaus Grossjohann
	Gesellschaft für Sozialen Fortschritt E.V.
	Münsterstrasse 17
	53 Bonn

Although both authors contributed to each chapter, Dr. Rix is primarily responsible for Chapters 1–4 and 11, and Dr. Fisher for Chapters 5–10. Chapter 12 was a joint effort.

Notes

CHAPTER 1

1. This line of reasoning is countered by assertions that (1) preventive health measures and a slowing down of the biological aging process prolong working life, and (2) changes in the methods of production minimize qualities that decrease with age and maximize strong characteristics of older workers (e.g., experience, judgment, reliability) that are of considerable significance in the fast-growing tertiary sector in Western Europe.

   These and other arguments (e.g., a trend toward a shrinking demand for labor due to the substitution of capital for labor) remain largely speculative, although plausible. Past experience offers insufficient quantitative proof that an increased percentage of older workers in the active labor force will substantially affect a nation's productivity and economic growth.

2. The confrontation of the sheer numbers of contributors to pensioners does not disclose the full effect of an aging population and work force on the social security system, if the latter is understood to protect the covered population against more than the loss of income due to retirement. Social security systems may also insure against the loss of income due to various forms of disability, industrial accidents, occupational diseases, unemployment, and sickness. Moreover, supplementary public assistance and social services may also be included in definitions of social security. Customarily, the term "social security" also covers family (child) allowances and health services. Many branches of social security will suffer reduced revenues and increased expenditures regardless of whether they are financed by contributions (payroll taxes) or general revenues derived from the taxpayers.

3. A commission of experts led by Helmut Meinhold is to report on the future of the German public pension program by 1983. Among the possible choices, the commission will have to choose between a rise in the contribution rate from 18.5 percent to 22 or even 32 percent and the capping of the pension (*Der Spiegel*, vol. 25, June 15, 1981).

4. For a description of the study, see Appendix A.

5. President Mitterand of France appears to favor a reduction of retirement age to 60 for men ("French Bosses Meet Their New Patron," 1981).

CHAPTER 2

1. The net-reproduction rate refers to the number of live girls born to one mother. According to the German report, "it assumes that during the mother's life, the number of births for specific age groups and the mortality rates in a given period of time continue to operate. The size of the net-reproduction rate indicates whether a population, in view of the relevant mortality, reproduces itself or not" (Eichner and Grossjohann, 1980, p. 21).

2. Dependency ratios are discussed in Chapter 3.

3. For a discussion of health costs for the very old, see Fogarty (1980b). The plight of the very old, and of women, is also discussed in *The Economist*, February 21, 1981.

4. We do not mean to imply that improvements in life expectancy can be measured precisely over the short run, but merely that short-run, unanticipated improvements can further aggravate demands on pension systems.

CHAPTER 3

1. Definitions of old and young dependents vary across countries; the footnotes to table 3.1 describe these differences.
2. Paillat, in comments on a draft of this book.
3. GNP projections for Denmark assume an annual growth rate of 3.5 percent during 1979–1990 and of 3 percent during 1990–2000.
4. Hilde Wander (1978, pp. 57–58) contends that "at current mortality and current standards of consumption, educational performance, and social security in the Federal Republic of Germany, it costs society about one-fourth to one-third more to bring up an average child from birth to age 20 than to support an average person of age 60 over the rest of his or her life." Wander's statement "refers to final private and public consumption expenditures," as well as to relevant fixed capital formation. The point that Wander stresses is that the period of time spent in dependency—20 versus 13 years—is substantially different.
5. Familial dependency costs may also include expenditures for aged family members (e.g., housing, food, clothing, nursing care, direct financial assistance) that are not reflected in public support estimates.
6. The two German models also assume that (1) the inflation rate does not exceed that of the 1970s; (2) the ratio of the government subsidy to total social security expenditures remains at the 1979 level; (3) the ratio of the labor force to the population aged 19–59 remains stable, and (4) that other conditions, especially the propensity to save and invest, remain unchanged.
7. The Swedish report does not address the youth offset argument in any detail. It notes merely that the middle fertility rate, rather than a higher one, may hold true. If so, the number of youth would be reduced by some 22 percent between 1975 and 2025. "In the short run, this would entail reduced costs for the child and youth groups, thus leaving economic resources to support the pensioners" (Berglind and Bergroth, 1980, p. 43).
8. The French report points out the disastrous effect of high unemployment on pension systems: the number of contributors (and hence, the amount of contributions) declines, while the number of pensioners continues to increase (Paillat and Chesnais, 1980). According to Eichner and Grossjohann (1980), a decrease of 200,000 in the number of employed reduces pension insurance revenues in Germany by DM 1 billion.

CHAPTER 4

1. When pension systems are financed by general revenues, all taxpayers, of course, and not only insured workers, bear the burden.
2. Labor force participation rates also include the unemployed who, in many countries, do not make contributions to retirement income systems. (Among the exceptions is West Germany.)
3. Under the severance pay scheme, members of unemployment funds between the ages of 60 and 66 have the right to receive severance pay if certain conditions are fulfilled. Both employed and unemployed persons are entitled to severance pay. According to Friis and Hansen (1980, p. 50), "severance pay has been designed as a scaling down of the unemployment level to the old-age pension level at the age of 67. During the first two and one-half years, the severance pay corresponds to the unemployment benefit rate, the following two years to 80 percent thereof, and then to 60 percent of the unemployment benefit rate." They note that this scheme may be regarded as a pension scheme, since only in exceptional cases is it expected that the recipient will return to employment. Because of the higher benefit level under severance pay, a "not inconsiderable substitution" between this and early retirement is likely to occur (Friis and Hansen, 1980).

4. These are: (1) the *zero alternative*, which assumes no change in the population in the labor force from 1983 on; (2) the *trend alternative*, which assumes no change in the labor force participation of men aged 16–44; a drop among men in the higher ages, and an increase among women whose rates will reach those of men by the year 2000; and (3) the *maximum alternative*, which implies that in the year 2000, labor force participation rates will be the same for men and women: 70 percent for ages 16–24, 97 percent for ages 25–64, and 10 percent among those 65–74 (Berglind and Bergroth, 1980).

5. The percentage of 60–64-year-old males claiming that they were retired rose from 6.0 to 11.6 between 1974 and 1978 (Fogarty, 1980b).

6. There is, Fogarty feels, reason to think that the improvement of occupational pensions will have a greater impact on early retirement in the future.

7. In comments on a draft of this manuscript, Dr. James Schulz of the National Retirement Income Policy Center at Brandeis University rightly points out that older workers may actually benefit from high unemployment rates if the country responds by liberalizing pension schemes. Under such circumstances, older workers would receive better pensions *without* paying higher taxes or contributions. The job release scheme in Denmark, we might mention, is clearly one example of how older workers might benefit during periods of high unemployment. While not a pension plan, it may be used as one (see note 3). Berglind and Bergroth (1980) note that the chief reason for the liberalization of legislation in 1970 and 1972 in Sweden was the difficulty older persons had in obtaining employment in a worsening labor market. Hence, legislators wanted to make it easier for persons 60 and older to leave the labor market. This, according to Berglind and Bergroth, is not a specifically Swedish phenomenon.

8. These trends in labor force participation are, at least partially, the result of structural changes. During the 1960s and up through the early 1970s, a sharp decline in self-employment occurred in Denmark. The self-employed have traditionally retired later and over a longer period of time. Schulz, in his review, also stresses the importance of discrimination and structural factors in contributing to the high unemployment rates of older workers, factors that were touched upon by most of the European co-researchers.

9. This ratio is, nonetheless, a more refined ratio than the one based on population statistics alone. Some accuracy is lost, however, because all elderly are assumed to be dependents.

CHAPTER 5

1. Another target of the tax revolt are the services to the aged. These services have assumed an important magnitude, particularly in Sweden, Denmark, and the United Kingdom. Since large parts of their costs are carried by the national governments, and hence, clearly visible in the budget and discussed in the legislature, they offer a target of opportunity for the tax revolt and a convenient target for the tax cutters. Where anti-inflationary policies require reduced government expenditures, appropriations for such programs as attendance assistance, home nursing, meals on wheels, etc. are deemed more vulnerable than old-age pensions (German Ministry of Labor). As relative latecomers among the government measures to assist the aged, they have increased faster in recent years than either pensions or health insurance costs. In Denmark (where services are not the focus of a tax revolt), they jumped between 1964/1965 and 1979 from 10.3 to 25.4 percent of total expenditures for the aged, while pension expenditures declined from 64.5 percent to 51.4 percent, and health expenditures from 25.2 to 23.2 percent.

2. That program encourages premature withdrawal from the labor market by tax-free allowances to employers in "assisted areas" who are within one year of the statutory pension age,

if they agree to leave their job early and if their employers agree to recruit another worker from the unemployment register.

3. The take-up in the Danish severance pay scheme was estimated at 17,000 persons; 45,000 workers took advantage of this measure.

4. Among those are: increasing availability and size of public and private pensions, increased assets, labor force participation of the spouse, bad health, and a host of hard-to-measure psychological and social attitudes such as aversion to the specific work, lack of advancement, poor working conditions, and peer behavior.

CHAPTER 6

1. This is reported from Sweden. The Swedish report states that this is based upon the fact that labor, which through political action was the main force in obtaining the pension laws, now has a stake in their existence and is willing to pay the costs (Berglind and Bergroth, 1980). Similar statements have been issued by union spokesmen in the United States.

2. It is, however, important to point out that the European co-researchers provide no solid documentation of a *widespread* tax revolt against the aged. Wander (1978) notes that at least up to the mid-1970s, the economies she examined managed to absorb the rising costs of care for the elderly.

3. As stated before, in France the payroll tax rate in the general system for old-age insurance increased by 27 percent between 1973 and 1978. The Swedes expect a 42 percent rise in the contribution rate within the next few years, from 12 percent of covered earnings in the wage-related second-tier pension program in 1980 to 17 percent in 1984. By 2020, depending on the underlying assumptions, this rate would jump to 25 or 34 percent. The current contribution rate in the United Kingdom is 16.5 percent. The Government Actuary estimated that this rate will need to increase by the turn of the century to 18.5 percent and stabilize when maturity of the system is reached at 20 percent of chargeable earnings. In the United States, the OASDI contribution, currently 10.8 percent of covered earnings, may rise by 2030 to 16 percent or 23 percent, again depending on the underlying assumptions.

4. In the case of occupational pensions in the United Kingdom, the Government Actuary estimates that funds would have to be accumulated at 7 percent for each 1 percent increase in real income if pension obligations in the year 2000 are to be met (Fogarty, 1980b).

5. Indexed bonds were held to violate the Gold Clause resolution of June 5, 1933 in the United States. After the latter's revocation in October 1977, a new obstacle appeared in the state usury laws (McCulloch, 1980).

6. This higher retirement pay is based on hours or time worked, rather than on earnings.

7. The German paper indicates that the unemployment rate of workers between 60 and 65 was more than double the general rate (6.5 percent versus 3.2 percent) and that the rate increased with increasing age (Eichner and Grossjohann, 1980).

8. This discussion should not be interpreted as denying that a pension program affects the economy and the labor market, or that the state of the economy and labor market requirements shape the pension program. (The long-term aspects of this interrelationship must be considered in the formulation of policy in each area and be expressed in the relevant measures taken.) It merely objects to short-term considerations in any of them governing long-term legislation upon which the expectations of the entire population rest. No European legislature would think it advisable to let a rash of business failures in a recession change the bankruptcy statute or the law of contracts.

9. Compensation for inflation has also been recalculated in Sweden. Heating oil and the cost of indirect taxes, such as the sales tax, are excluded from the index.
10. This partial pension is indexed, but the pay is not.

CHAPTER 7

1. Between 1883 and 1887, Otto von Bismark established a series of social security programs originally enabling manual workers alone to carry the risks of failing health, industrial accidents, and loss of income in old age. Administration of the old-age payment was now in the hands of the German state, wrested from the socialists and the unions. Retirement pay was determined by the size of the compulsory contribution levied in equal parts on workers and their employers. These contributions were closely related to the worker's earning up to a maximum. The system was patterned after voluntary, management-supported private insurance annuities. Later changes reflected lessons drawn from operational experience. Coverage was extended, the scope of protection widened, and full capital funding replaced by current financing based upon the intergenerational contract discussed in the text. In spite of these and other amendments, the system remains basically a social *insurance* system, tied to labor force participation and offering an earnings-related pension.

    The British Pension Act of 1925, with its contributory benefit for old age, widows, and orphans, proved inadequate to meet the demands of the wartime population. Inflation decreased the value of the retirement pension, as well as the financial basis of that and all other separate compulsory social insurance plans dealing with workmen's compensation (1897), health insurance (1912), and unemployment insurance (1912). The Committee on Reconstruction Problems invited Sir William H. Beveridge to review this area, which he did in his report entitled *Social Insurance and Allied Services* (London, 1942). Beveridge proposed a *unified* attack on want, whatever its cause, to protect all residents (universal coverage). They, together with their employers, if any, were to make a compulsory flat-rate contribution, which Parliament later changed to an earnings-related payment. In turn, they were to receive a uniform flat-rate benefit adequate to meet their minimum needs. Later legislative amendments allowed for variations in the pensions to different-sized families, but held fast on the basic equality and flat-rate nature of the pension available to aged in similar circumstances. Universal coverage and traces of the flat-rate pension can be seen even today in the United Kingdom's system. The unification principle lives on in the all-embracing definition of social security.

    The Beveridge Plan influenced programs in Canada, Scandinavia, and New Zealand, among others. The Bismarkian Social Insurance System underlies many older continental European, Latin American, and other systems, including that of the United States.
2. Five out of six earnings-related pensions are contracted out in the United Kingdom.
3. The creation of the general scheme did not affect the continuation of about 120 (small) special schemes.
4. Contributions to contracted-out pensions reduce taxable earnings; those to the state pension scheme do not. Returns on capital funds of the private schemes are tax free; those on private savings are generally taxable. An exception, as Fogarty notes in his comments on a draft of this manuscript, includes those private savings that take the form of contributions to a superannuation plan (e.g., for the self-employed). These savings are not taxable.
5. To gain perspective, the net annual increase in the size of private pension funds in the United Kingdom (1977) was £6 billion, while that of net national savings amounted to £10 billion.

6. Nor can government exercise any significant control over the private system's costs, which, due to proliferation of funds, are occasionally based on a very poor distribution of risks. Hence, they are, by their very nature, higher than those of a nationwide state system.
7. Miegel (1981) estimates that the net value of the West German population's home ownership and rental property amounted to DM 2.2 billion German.

CHAPTER 8

1. Fogarty notes, however, that existing commitments regarding price indexing of social security benefits, an increase in the amount of guaranteed earnings-related pensions under the Act of 1975, as well as the increasing of the availability of occupational pensions—even if eroded, are likely to have the opposite effect for the United Kingdom. (Fogarty made this point in commenting on the draft of this book.)

CHAPTER 9

1. The reports warn against such a move as leading merely to "more years of poverty" and leading to "debilitating leisure." Fogarty (1980b, p. 141) observes that "forced labour for the aged is hardly a slogan on which any political party is likely to go to the country."
2. France, in contrast to Denmark, Sweden, the United Kingdom, and West Germany, keeps a relatively high proportion of its postretirement-age workers employed in certain industries. The others insist on their retirement.
3. According to Fogarty (in comments on the draft of this book), the latest estimates (which may be overestimates) for the net cost of abolishing the earnings test for the first five years after standard retirement ages is about £45–50 million a year.
4. It has been the United Kingdom experience that the creation of part-time jobs has little to do with subsidies, but a great deal to do with general level of employment (Fogarty, in comments on the draft of this book).

CHAPTER 10

1. For employers, the retirement age means a final stop to an employment contract binding them and their employees. It obviates firing of superannuated, less productive workers, and makes room for reorganization, modernization of production, and hiring of young, less costly workers. In consequence, most private pension plans contain a mandatory retirement age, as well as provisions for early retirement.
2. On the uncertainty of long-range projections, see Robert Ball, 1980.
3. Fogarty, in comments on the draft of this book. The study mentioned was conducted by the Policy Studies Institute.
4. The British Trades Union Congress (TUC), the major voice for organized labor in the United Kingdom, is a roof organization of the most important labor organizations, and comparable to the AFL-CIO. French union federations are divided by political affiliation. Confédération Générale du Travail (CGT) is the central organization of the community-oriented unions, composed mainly of manual workers in France. It has the largest membership. The union of higher managerial and technical workers, the Confédération Générale des Cadres (CGC),

which understandably holds different views on retirement age, is the exception. As a federation, it is not tied to a political party.

CHAPTER 11

1. Jeff Clair contributed substantially to this chapter.
2. Between 1965 and 1975 alone, for example, death rates among the 85-and-older population declined by 25 percent.
3. Fifty-one percent of all full-time private wage and salary workers were covered by a pension plan in 1979; 48 percent were vested.
4. This is a semi-independent body with members from business, organized labor, academia, and the general public.
5. Not all commissioners agreed with this recommendation. One warned against the differential impact that a higher retirement age would have on different classes of workers. The lower paid, with greater health problems and a lower life expectancy, would be especially hurt by this change. Another argued that this modification would "break faith with younger workers" (President's Commission on Pension Policy, 1981, p. 64).
6. This figure would increase for each additional year of continued employment; a person who retired at 63 years and 8 months would have received the 80 percent he or she now receives at 62.
7. A maximum earner retiring at age 65 in 1987 would have seen his or her benefits reduced by 9 percent.
8. There is a general consensus that the social security system will continue to meet the major part of its commitment to the present generation of retired persons. Social security benefits will also be paid to retirees in the foreseeable future. What remains in question is whether the system will continue to be financed solely, or even primarily, by payroll taxes. In the short run, at least, supplemental funds or loans from general revenues, sizable interfund transfers, tax increases, or some other source will be necessary to pay those promised benefits.

   To substitute general revenues for social security contributions could indirectly lead to changes in the practice of granting benefits by right. General revenues are subject to the yearly process of budgetary review. Income taxes are appropriated as Congress sees fit, and the worker has no guarantee that they will be used for social security or any other program. There is some concern that use of general revenues would undermine the confidence in social security as an earned right of the insured.

References

COUNTRY REPORTS PREPARED FOR THE AMERICAN INSTITUTES FOR RESEARCH INTERNATIONAL RETIREMENT-AGE POLICY PROJECT

Benjamin, Bernard, and Overton, Elizabeth. *The Prospects for Mortality Decline in England and Wales.* Supplement to working paper by Michael Fogarty. London: Policy Studies Institute, 1980.

Berglind, Hans, and Bergroth, Alf. *Retirement and Retirement Age in Sweden.* Working paper for a seminar of policymakers, March 27, 1980, and report on the seminar. Stockholm: University of Stockholm, 1980.

Eichner, Harald, and Grossjohann, Klaus. *Demographic, Biomedical, and Economic Influences on Future Retirement-Age Policies.* Working paper for a seminar of policymakers, April 1980, and report on the seminar. Bonn: Gesellschaft für Sozialen Fortschritt E.V., 1980.

Fogarty, Michael P. *The Future of Retirement Pensions and Retirement Age in Britain.* Working paper for a seminar of policymakers, March 31, 1980, and report on the seminar. London: Policy Studies Institute, 1980a.

Friis, Henning, and Hansen, Per Vejrup. *Pensions and Retirements up to the Year 2000.* Working paper for a seminar of policymakers, March 24, 1980, and minutes of the seminar. Copenhagen: The Danish National Institute of Social Research, 1980.

Paillat, Paul, and Chesnais, Jean-Claude. *Retirement and Pensions in France: Outlook and Prospects.* Working paper for a seminar of policymakers, April 16–17, 1980, and report on the seminar. Paris: National Institute for Demographic Studies, 1980.

Rix, Sara E., and Clair, Jeff. *Retirement-Age Policy in the United States.* Washington, D.C.: American Institutes for Research, 1981.

ADDITIONAL REFERENCES

Advisory Council on Social Security. "Social Security Financing and Benefits." Reports of the 1979 Advisory Council on Social Security. Mimeographed. Washington, D.C., 1979.

Alber, Jens. "A Crisis of the Welfare State? The Case of West Germany." Paper presented at a conference of the European Center for Political Research, Florence, Italy, March 1980.

American Council of Life Insurance. *Map '78: Monitoring the Attitudes of the Public.* Washington, D.C.: American Council of Life Insurance, 1978.

American Council of Life Insurance. *Map '79: Monitoring the Attitudes of the Public.* Washington, D.C.: American Council of Life Insurance, 1979.

Ball, Robert. "Social Security: Today and Tomorrow." Testimony before the United States Senate Special Committee on Aging, November 21, 1980.

Bayo, Francisco R., and Faber, Joseph F. *Population Projections for OASDI Cost Estimates, 1980.* Washington, D.C.: U.S. Department of Health and Human Services, Social Security Administration, Office of the Actuary, June 1980.

Berglind, Hans. "Increased Early Retirement, Reasons, Consequences, and Lessons." in Carl Ström and Yngve Zotterman, eds., *The Conditions of the Elderly—How Are Resources to Be Distributed?* Stockholm: Liberförlag, 1978 (in Swedish, cited in Berglind and Bergroth, 1980).

Blanchard, Francis. "Social Security on the Crossroads." *International Labor Review* 119, 2 (March–April 1980).

Causey, Mike. "The Federal Diary." *Washington Post*, May 20, 1981.

Clark, Robert. "The Influence of Low Fertility Rates and Retirement Policy on Dependency Costs." Paper prepared for a conference on retirement-age policy, American Institutes for Research, Washington, D.C., 1976.

Commissariat Général du Plan. *Vieillir demain.* Rapport du Groupe, "Prospective personnes âgées," Preparation du 8ieme Plan 1981–1985, La Documentation Française, March 1980.

Commission of the European Communities (EEC). *Social Accounts.* Luxumburg: Statistical Office of the European Communities, 1977 and 1980.

Commission of the European Communities (EEC). *Attitude of the Working Population to Retirement.* Brussels: EEC, May 1978a.

Commission of the European Communities (EEC). *The Economic Implications of Demographic Change in the European Community: 1975–1995, Part I: Report.* Brussels: EEC, June 1978b.

Crona, Goran. "Partial Retirement in Sweden—Developments and Experiences." Revised version of a paper prepared for the 1979 International Sociological Association Meetings, March 1980.

Davies, B. Statement prepared for AFL-CIO Pension Fund Seminar. Washington, D.C.: George Meany Center for Labor Studies, January 22, 1981.

Derthick, Martha. *Policy for Social Security.* Washington, D.C.: The Brookings Institution, 1979.

Ehrbar, A. F. "How to Save Social Security." *Fortune*, August 25, 1980.

Employee Benefit Research Institute. *Retirement Income Policy: Considerations for Effective Decisionmaking.* Washington, D.C.: Employee Benefit Research Institute, 1980.

Espenshade, Thomas J. "The Value and Cost of Raising Children." *Population Bulletin* 32 (1977).

Espenshade, Thomas J. "Raising a Child Can Now Cost $85,000." *Intercom* 8 (September 1980).

Fisher, Paul. "The Social Security Crisis—An International Dilemma." *Aging and Work*, Winter 1978.

Fogarty, Michael. *Retirement-Age and Retirement Costs—The Long-Term Challenge.* London: Policy Studies Institute Report, 1980b (draft).

"French Bosses Meet Their New Patron." *The Economist* 297 (June 6, 1981).

Geiger, Theodore, assisted by Frances M. Geiger. *Welfare and Efficiency: Their Interactions in Western Europe and Implications for International Economic Relations.* Washington, D.C.: National Planning Association, 1978.

Gustaitis, Rosa. "Old vs. Young in Florida: Review of an Aging America." *Saturday Review*, February 16, 1980.

Gutchess, Jocelyn. "Pension Investment: The European Model." AFL-CIO *Federationist*, June 1980a.

Gutchess, Jocelyn. "Can Union Pension Funds Serve Dual Purposes? The Experience in Sweden and Denmark." Paper presented before the President's Commission on Pension Policy, Washington, D.C., October 23, 1980b.

Haanes-Olsen, Leif. "Earnings Replacement Rates of Old-Age Benefits 1965–1975." *Social Security Bulletin*, January 1978.

Harris, Louis, and Associates. *American Attitudes Toward Pensions and Retirement.* Hearing before the Select Committee on Aging, U.S. Congress, February 28, 1979. Washington, D.C.: U.S. Government Printing Office, 1979.

Harris, Louis, and Associates. *ABC News–Harris Survey*. June 1980.

Hart Research Associates, Peter D. *A Nationwide Survey of Attitudes Toward Social Security*. Report prepared for the National Commission on Social Security, Washington, D.C., 1980.

Horlick, Max. "The Earnings Replacement Rate of Old-Age Benefits: An International Comparison." *Social Security Bulletin*, March 1970.

Horlick, Max. "The Impact of an Aging Population on Social Security: The Foreign Experience." In *Social Security in a Changing World*. Washington, D.C.: U.S. Department of Health, Education and Welfare, Social Security Administration, September 1979.

"Innovations in Working Patterns." *Transatlantic Perspectives*, June 1981.

International Labour Office (ILO). *Labor Force Estimates and Projections 1950–2000*. Geneva: ILO, 1977.

International Labour Office (ILO). *The Cost of Social Security 1972–1974*. Geneva: ILO, 1979a.

International Labour Office (ILO). *Older Workers, Work and Retirement*. Report 6. Geneva: ILO, 1979b.

International Social Security Association (ISSA). *Implications for Social Security of Research on Aging and Retirement*. ISSA Studies and Research no. 9. Geneva: ISSA, 1977.

International Social Security Association (ISSA). *Problems of Social Security Under Economic Recession and Inflation*. ISSA Studies and Research no. 10. Geneva: ISSA, 1978.

International Social Security Association (ISSA). *Social Protection and the Over-75s*. ISSA Studies and Research no. 12. Geneva: ISSA, 1979a.

International Social Security Association (ISSA). *Retirement Age Practices in Ten Industrial Societies 1960–1976*. ISSA Studies and Research no. 14. Geneva: ISSA, 1979b.

Jacobs, Andy. *Social Security Financing Issues*. Hearing before the Subcommittee on Social Security of the House Committee on Ways and Means, U.S. Congress, September 28, 1979.

Keyflitz, Nathan, and Flieger, Wilhelm. *World Population: An Analysis of Vital Data*. Chicago: University of Chicago Press, 1968.

McCulloch, J. Huston. "The Ban on Indexed Bonds, 1933–77." *American Economic Review*, December 1980.

Miegel, Meinhard. *Sicherheit im Alter: Plädoyer für die Wieterentwicklung des Rentensystems*. IWG-Impulse, Schriften des Instituts für Wirtschafts- und Gesellschaftspolitik, IWG, Bonn. Stuttgart: Verlag BONN AKTUELL, 1981.

Morrison, Malcolm. "International Developments in Retirement Flexibility." *Aging and Work*, Fall 1979.

National Commission on Social Security. *Social Security in America's Future*. Washington, D.C.: National Commission on Social Security, 1981.

Organization for Economic Cooperation and Development (OECD), Directorate for Social Affairs, Manpower, and Education. *Socio-Economic Policies for the Elderly: Questionnaire and Analytical Synthesis Report*, SME/SAIR/E/80.02. May 19, 1980 (provisional translation).

Otero, J. F. "Immigration Policy: Drifting Toward Disaster." AFL-CIO *Federationist*, February 1981.

Parnes, Herbert L.; Nestel, Gilbert; Chirikos, Thomas N.; Daymont, Thomas N.; Mott, Frank L.; Parsons, Donald O.; and Associates. *From the Middle to the Later Years: Longitudinal Studies of the Pre- and Post-Retirement Experiences of Men*. A publication of the Center for Human Resource Research, Ohio State University, May 1979 (published in revised form by MIT Press, 1981).

Population Reference Bureau (PRB). *World Population Data Sheet*. Washington, D.C.: PRB, 1979, 1980, 1981.

President's Commission on Pension Policy. *An Interim Report*. Washington, D.C.: President's Commission on Pension Policy, 1980a.

President's Commission on Pension Policy. *Preliminary Findings of a Nationwide Survey on*

Retirement Income Issues. Washington, D.C.: President's Commission on Pension Policy, 1980b.

President's Commission on Pension Policy. *Coming of Age: Toward a National Retirement Income Policy.* Washington, D.C.: President's Commission on Pension Policy, 1981.

Rohrlich, George. "International Perspectives on Social Security," Special Study on Economic Change. In *Social Security and Pensions: Programs of Equity and Security*, vol. 8. Washington, D.C.: U.S. Congress Joint Economic Committee, December 4, 1980.

Ross, Stanford G. "Social Security: a Worldwide Issue." *Social Security Bulletin*, August 1979a.

Ross, Stanford G. "Social Security in a Changing World." *HEW-SSA Report* 79–119–8, September 1979b.

Samuelson, Robert J. "Whatever Happened to the Promise of An Ever-Expanding Economy." *National Journal*, January 19, 1980.

Schulz, James. *Assessing the Adequacy of Pension Income.* Testimony before the President's Commission on Pension Policy, Washington, D.C., January 11, 1980a.

Schulz, James. *The Economics of Aging.* Belmont, Calif.: Wadsworth, 1980b.

Sheppard, Harold L. "Current and Future Retirement-Age Policy In Five Western European Countries and the United States." Proposal submitted to the German Marshall Fund of the United States, September 1978.

Sheppard, Harold L., and Rix, Sara E. *The Graying of Working America.* New York: The Free Press, 1977.

Smith, Geoffrey. "Britain Cuts Indexing of Government Benefits." *Journal of the Institute for Socioeconomic Studies*, Summer 1980.

Spant, R. Statement prepared for AFL-CIO Pension Fund Seminar. Washington, D.C.: George Meany Center for Labor Studies, January 22, 1981.

Stein, Bruno. *Social Security and Pensions in Transition.* New York: The Free Press, 1980.

"Tax Burdens Around the World." *Aging International* 6 (Spring 1979).

Taylor, Paul. *Social Policy in the European Communities: A Preliminary Examination of the Present Crisis.* Paper presented at a meeting of the European Consortium for Political and Social Research, Florence, Italy, March 1980.

Thurow, Lester. "Undamning the American Economy." *New York Times Magazine*, May 3, 1981.

Torrey, Barbara Boyle, and Thompson, Carole J. *An International Comparison of Pension Systems.* Washington, D.C.: President's Commission on Pension Policy, 1980.

Tracy, Martin B. "Maintaining the Value of Social Security Benefits During Inflation: Foreign Experience." *Social Security Bulletin*, November 1976a.

Tracy, Martin B. "World Developments and Trends in Social Security." *Social Security Bulletin*, April 1976b.

Tracy, Martin B. "Flexible Retirement Features Abroad." *Social Security Bulletin*, May 1978.

Tracy, Martin B. "Trends in Retirement." *International Social Security Review*, year 32, no. 2, 1979.

United Nations. *Demographic Yearbook.* New York: United Nations Department of Economic and Social Affairs, 1967, 1968, 1970, 1972, and 1978.

United Nations. *Selected World Demographic Indicators by Countries, 1950–2000.* New York: United Nations, Population Division, 1975.

U.S. Department of Health, Education, and Welfare. *Social Security and the Changing Roles of Men and Women.* Washington, D.C.: U.S. Government Printing Office, 1979.

U.S. Department of Health, Education, and Welfare (HEW), Social Security Administration (SSA). *Social Security Programs Throughout the World.* HHS-SSA, Office of Policy, Office of Research and Statistics, Research Report no. 54, SSA Publication 13-11805, 1979, revised May 1980.

U.S. Department of Labor and U.S. Department of Health and Human Services. *Employment and Training Report of the President.* Washington, D.C.: U.S. Government Printing Office, 1980.

Wander, Hilde. "Zero Population Growth Now: The Lessons from Europe." In T. J. Espenshade and W. J. Serow, eds., *The Economic Consequences of Slowing Population Growth.* New York: Academic Press, 1978, pp. 41–69.

"World Leaders in Part-time Employment." *Sweden Now,* vol. 14, Special Issue, 1980.

Index

About the Authors

Sara E. Rix, who holds a Ph.D. in sociology from the University of Virginia, has recently joined the Research and Education Institute of the Congressional Caucus for Women's Issues, where she is involved in establishing a systematic linkage between researchers of women's issues and federal policymakers.

Prior to joining the institute in January 1981, Dr. Rix was a research scientist with the American Institutes for Research in Washington, D.C. Her primary research interests are directed toward the economics of aging, retirement-age policy, and the employment policies of older workers.

Dr. Rix was a consultant to the 1981 White House Conference on Aging technical committees on employment and on older persons as a resource. In addition to belonging to several professional associations, she consults regularly in the area of older-worker employment and retirement problems. Dr. Rix coauthored with Dr. Harold Sheppard *The Graying of Working America*.

Paul Fisher holds a J.D. from the University of Vienna. He is a consultant in international economics whose areas of expertise include pensions, health insurance, and manpower policy. Dr. Fisher's most recent consultancy was with the American Institutes for Research in Washington, D.C. He is an associate at the Bureau of Applied Research at Columbia University and a member of the Editorial Advisory Board of *Aging and Work*, a publication of the National Council on the Aging. He has also served as an advisor to the President's Commission on Pension Policy.

Dr. Fisher was chief, international staff, of the Office of External Affairs in the Social Security Administration from 1963 to 1968 and from 1969 to 1978. Among many other activities, Dr. Fisher has served as a health-insurance consultant to Korean government agencies and the Agency for International Development; consultant on social security to the Korean program of Harvard University's Development Assistance Service; senior research economist with the International Labour Office in Geneva; and deputy chief of the Planning Assistance Division's program coordination staff of AID. He also taught economics for many years.

About the Co-Researchers

DENMARK: **Henning Friis,** an economist with a degree from the University of Copenhagen, was social science advisor to the Danish Ministries of Social Affairs and Labour from 1941 to 1958 and executive director of the Danish National Institute of Social Research from 1958 to 1979. His numerous international activities include serving as chairman of the Social Science Committee of the International Gerontological Association, director of an EEC study on Poverty and Policies Against Poverty in Denmark, a member of the International Social Science Council, a WHO consultant on Care of the Elderly, and director of seminars of the UN and UNESCO on social planning, welfare of the aged, and social-science policy. *Old People in Three Industrial Societies* (coauthor) and *The Aged in Denmark: Social Programmes* are two of his many publications.

Per Vejrup Hansen holds a M.Sc. degree from the University of Copenhagen. From 1970 to 1977, Mr. Hansen was a junior lecturer in economic theory and economic history at the University of Copenhagen, after which he was employed by the Statistical Bureau of Denmark in the Department of Population and Vital Statistics. Since 1980, he has been a research assistant with the Danish National Institute of Social Research (Section of Labour Market Research).

FRANCE: **Paul Paillat** has been a research officer with the National Institute for Demographic Studies in Paris since 1956. He is now head of the Department of Social Demography at the institute. Mr. Paillat holds a doctorate in political economy from the University of Paris. He has served as chairman of the French Society of Gerontology, as a member of a WHO panel of experts, as scientific advisor to the French Foundation of Gerontology, and general secretary (rapporteur) of the Commissariat du Plan's working group on gerontological issues. Mr. Paillat has lectured extensively and has served as an organizer and chairman of several international seminars on aging issues.

Jean-Claude Chesnais, who has a Ph.D. in economics, was a collaborator of Sauvy at the Centre national de la Recherche Scientifique from 1971 to 1975, after which he moved to the National Institute for Demographic Studies. He has been a member of a group examining aging problems at the Commissariat Général du Plan. He has written on employment and unemployment issues; socioeconomic inequalities and the life cycle; consumption pattern forecasts; and various implications of aging.

SWEDEN: **Hans E. Berglind**, Ph.D. (sociology), is a professor of social work at the University of Stockholm. Prior to coming to the University of Stockholm as an associate professor of sociology in 1970, Mr. Berglind was an ILO expert (human relations) at the Hungarian Management Development Center in Budapest. He had previously held a variety of teaching and managerial posts. His extensive publications include writings on pensions and work; aging; mobility and participation in the Swedish labor force; and working conditions, employment, and labor market policy.

Alf Bergroth, who also holds a Ph.D. in sociology, has worked as a social worker in Swedish welfare agencies. He is presently employed as senior lecturer in social legislation at the University of Östersund in northern Sweden. Mr. Bergroth has conducted research in the areas of social services and retirement.

UNITED KINGDOM: **Michael Fogarty**, who holds an MA degree from Oxford University, is affiliated with the Policy Studies Institute in London. He has held the position of senior fellow at the Centre for Studies in Social Policy and visiting fellow and associate professor, Administrative Staff College, Henley. He has also held a number of other academic and research positions and has served as assistant editor of *The Economist*. He has been a member of a number of commissions and committees of inquiry, including the Commission on the Status of Women (Ireland), the Commission on the Insurance Industry (Ireland), and the Committee on Aid to Political Parties. Mr. Fogarty has also been involved as an expert or member in international conferences and commissions. He has published in the areas of town planning and location of industry; general economics; industrial relations and company law; women and work; politics and social movements; and pension policy.

WEST GERMANY: **Harald Eichner** is director of the Gesellschaft für Sozialen Fortschritt in Bonn, a position he has held since 1973. Previously, Mr. Eichner was an assistant at the Gesellschaft. He has studied law at the Universities of Cologne and Berlin, and political science and history at the University of Berlin. He holds a Diploma of Political Science. Research interests and publications encompass the areas of health policy (health insurance, preventive medicine, and health economics); educational policy; labor market policy; and population policy.

Klaus Grossjohann, who has a Diploma of Sociology, is a member of the research team of the Gesellschaft für Sozialen Fortschritt in Bonn. Fields of study include sociology, social psychology, and economics. Recent research interests are in the areas of health policy (preventive medicine), the social security system, gerontology, and demography.